CHILDREN DREAMING
Pictures in my pillow

BRENDA MALLON

PENGUIN BOOKS

PENGUIN BOOKS

Published by the Penguin Group
27 Wrights Lane, London w8 5TZ, England
Viking Penguin Inc., 40 West 23rd Street, New York, New York 10010, USA
Penguin Books Australia Ltd, Ringwood, Victoria, Australia
Penguin Books Canada Ltd, 2801 John Street, Markham, Ontario, Canada L3R 1B4
Penguin Books (NZ) Ltd, 182–190 Wairau Road, Auckland 10, New Zealand

Penguin Books Ltd, Registered Offices: Harmondsworth, Middlesex, England

First published 1989
10 9 8 7 6 5 4 3 2 1

Made and printed in Great Britain by
Richard Clay Ltd, Bungay, Suffolk
Filmset in Monophoto Sabon

To my children, Karl, Crystal and Danny

Contents

Introduction

There you are, fast asleep and dreaming, when from your slumbers you are rudely awoken: the accustomed lot of parents of young children, residential care workers or indeed anyone who cares for young children. Those who live or work with older children might find that it is sleep-walking or nightmares that give cause for concern. Whether young or old, we all dream, and childhood dreams are particularly important and revealing.

I was asked to write a book about children's dreams by many mothers who took part in the research for my last book *Women Dreaming*. While carrying out hundreds of interviews, I was struck by the fact that childhood dreams were remembered and talked about as if they had happened yesterday. The fear, the fun, the terror were felt now – back again after all the years. The women also wanted to know how to help their children with dreams, how to bring calm after a terrifying nightmare, and to understand themselves what might be at the root of distressing dreams.

About the same time, my own toddlers began wailing from nightmares or told me tales about magical magicians who came to their room when they were asleep. At breakfast I was interested; at three in the morning all I wanted to do was to get them back to sleep so I could return to my cosy, oh-so-far-away bed! At three in the morning it is difficult to be other than dismissive. However, I learnt from my children that their dreams were not to be taken lightly.

As a counsellor and consultant working with children and with professionals responsible for the welfare of young people –

teachers, social workers, doctors, nurses and others – I wanted to look at ways in which dreams tell us about the feelings and fears of children. And the only place to start was with the children themselves.

I contacted nurseries, schools, youth organizations, hospitals – anywhere that children might be found who would willingly, and with their parents' consent, agree to answer questions about their dreams. With little ones, those aged 3 to 6, I collected their drawings and taped what they had to say. Children who could read and write had individual, confidential questionnaires to complete (a copy of the questionnaire follows this introduction). All who took part were promised total secrecy.

The children revealed amazing insights into what they thought dreams were – hence the sub-title 'Pictures in my Pillow' – and provided a wealth of information about the way in which dreams mirror individual development. Dreams also show how our children are hampered by fears and what they want adults to do about them. I hope this book will help anyone who cares about children to feel more confident in exploring the world of dreams, and so, indirectly, that it will give support to those children who feel so powerless in the face of unhappy dreams.

I have arranged the book so that the theory of dreams and dreaming come in the first chapter, followed by three chapters showing how dreams change from birth to 16. You choose what parts are important for you at present – the book can be dipped into and does not have to be read sequentially. In order to maintain balance and avoid sexist language, 'he' and 'she' have been alternated between consecutive chapters. Finally, you will find a list of books for children, which will be an enjoyable way of delving into the treasure house of dreams.

Brenda Mallon
January 1989

Questionnaire

BRENDA MALLON M.ED.
CRESCENT VILLA
20 CIRCULAR ROAD
MANCHESTER M20 9LP

COUNSELLOR AND STAFF DEVELOPMENT CONSULTANT

DREAMS OF CHILDHOOD

I am writing a book on dreams which will be published by Penguin. You can help by answering these questions. If you are over 16 please write what you remember of your childhood dreams. All replies will be treated in confidence and I will let you know when the book will be in the bookshops. (Use more paper if you haven't enough space!)

Name:
Address:
Age:

What do you dream about?
What is the most frightening dream you have had?
What is the happiest dream you have had?
What kind of dreams do you have when you are ill?
Do you have any TV or book characters in your dreams?
Do you talk to anyone about your dreams?
Have you ever had a dream about war or bombs?
If you have nightmares please tell me about them.
Why do you think we dream?
Is there anything else you can think of that I should put in the book?
Put any more dream examples in the space provided – drawings too if you like.
Please tell me about yourself and your life.
Finally, do you want me to use your name or shall I keep it a secret?
Please return this to me. Thank you!

Brenda Mallon

ONE

Why Do Children Dream?

'Pictures in my pillow' is how 4-year-old Eve explained her dreams. She didn't think she created those dreams but that they were in her pillow and came to her at night. Like other children, and adults, she was both fascinated by and a bit afraid of her dreams. As she grows older her explanation will undoubtedly change. She will begin to understand the process that is involved in dreaming and the source of dreams. But along the way she will ask, as so many of us have, 'Why do we dream?'

Before we address that question we need to find out about dreaming in relation to sleep. Sleep is a progression of repeated cycles, involving different phases of brain and body activity. From recordings of brainwaves, blood pressure, pulse, temperature changes and biochemical changes we have found that, at regular intervals, the sleeper enters a state that resembles her most alert waking moment, yet paradoxically her muscles seem almost paralysed.

The electroencephalographs used in well-documented sleep research produce EEG readings which tell us that as we drift into sleep there may be sensations of falling; 'myclonic' jerks may occur in which the sleeper feels she has fallen off a kerb for instance. This is followed by Stage-1 sleep where muscles relax and heart rate slows down. Stage-2 sleep shows quick bursts of brain activity, known as 'spindles', as the sleeper goes deeper into sleep. At this stage even with eyes open, or with a bright light shining inches from her face, the dreamer will be functionally blind. In Stage-3 sleep the spindles change and large slow brainwaves occur, the heart rate continues to slow down and the body temperature and blood pressure drop. When we

Meg (11)

reach Stage-4 sleep, often known as delta sleep because of the large brainwaves of that name, the sleeper is almost immobile and very hard to rouse. If a child is to wet the bed or sleep-walk, she is likely to do it in this deep sleep.

Rapid Eye Movement (REM) sleep occurs in Stage-5 sleep. REM phases tell us that dreaming is taking place; eyes move rapidly beneath closed lids as if watching a film. The body shows increased tension, oxygen consumption increases and the adrenal glands pour hormones into the system as if preparing for action; the action is Stage-1 REM, which lasts about ten minutes. But despite this storm of activity in body and mind the dreamer may be unusually still. Her body muscles generally go limp. If wakened in this REM stage, dreams will be reported. These cycles of quiescence, interspersed with intense activity of the brain, happen at sixty- to ninety-minute intervals, though the REM period itself may last for twenty minutes or so. Such sleep stages are repeated four or five times. Towards morning the REM phases become more vivid and elaborate.

Though these cycles may vary slightly from individual to

individual, they form our basic sleep pattern and continue through the night. In all, we spend about six years of our life in this remarkable condition interchangeably known as dreaming, REM sleep or paradoxical sleep. But to return to the question we set off to answer – why do we dream?

The answer is that dreaming has a number of vital functions. The children and adolescents who took part in my research knew what these were, and though the language used was not particularly sophisticated – they didn't use scientific terms – their essential grasp of the significance of dreaming cannot be faulted. Let them lead us down the path of understanding. Maybe you will recognize your child, or yourself, here.

Dreams help restore our brains

Camille (7):

> I think we go into the land of dreams because our brain switches off . . . it has a rest . . . it relaxes.

At Edinburgh University, Professor Ian Oswald, when research-ing the effects of drugs such as barbiturates on sleep, discovered that dream sleep was suppressed by many drugs but that once the drugs were no longer administered there was a rebound period of compensation when paradoxical sleep increased mas-sively. This lasted about eight weeks, which is the approximate time needed to repair brain cells. He concluded that through dream sleep the brain renews itself. Some drugs prevent such a renewal taking place and so the brain valiantly tries to make up the deficit by dreaming avidly once the drugs are stopped. You may find that your child or the children you work with talk about episodes of 'excessive dreaming'. If so, consider whether medication may be linked in some way.

Our brains cannot rest while we are awake, even if we lie quietly in a darkened room, for when we are awake we are in a state of 'quiet readiness', prepared to act if need be. Only when the brain is 'off line', that is when we sleep, can it rest and be restored. The wear and tear of waking life needs to be repaired in sleep. The dream state can then be seen as a means of recuperation where the neural systems involved in learning, memory, attention and emotional activities are renewed.

Brian (13), a rugby fanatic from Widnes, told me: 'We dream so that we don't get fed up while we're asleep.' For him dreaming is a sort of in-house entertainment system! It helps him relax. Like many children, he was quite adamant that we dream in order to prevent boredom.

Dreams sort out the events of our day

Roxanne (16) described a very important aspect of dreaming when she said:

> I am sure dreaming is a way of getting rid of all the loose ends of thoughts in our minds. I usually find that I can connect my dreams with something which has recently happened or with something I have seen or heard.

This is indeed an important reason for dreaming.

When I first met Ilse (9), after a playground fight, she had her head down, bottom lip out and was aggressively foot-tapping, waiting outside the headteacher's office. Later in the day I caught up with her and we talked about dreams. She told me that what happened to her during the day influenced her dreams. So, sanguinely: 'I got into trouble today, and I'll dream about it tonight.'

These girls recognized the way in which dreams echo daily events. They have a very good working hypothesis about why we dream. The scientific reasoning behind this is to be found in the 'Computer Theory'. It was first described by psychologist Dr Christopher Evans. He suggests that what is known as paradoxical sleep allows vital processing of data to take place. In dreaming, the brain – the human computer – goes 'off line' and analyses, sorts, classifies and interprets the mass of information and stimuli which flood through our senses every minute of the day. Out-of-date information is updated, while irrelevant data is reclassified. All this cannot be done while we are awake because too much information is coming in constantly and we have to deal with it there and then. People who meditate or deliberately remove themselves from distractions can do some of this work while they are still 'on line', but most of us do not allow time for that, so it is up to our dreams to do it for us.

While we dream the brain attempts to interpret data. As evidence to support his theory Dr Evans points out that newly born babies spend up to sixteen out of twenty-four hours asleep, half of which is in paradoxical sleep, while adults spend only 20 per cent of eight hours' sleep in dream sleep. Such long periods are needed so that babies' brains can come to terms with the vast array of stimuli coming from their brand new world.

Rosemary (13), from London, believes that 'dreaming helps us get far-back thoughts which are remote and distant in our minds'. She has recognized that through dreams we can get in touch with memories and experiences which are suppressed during our waking life. However, if we are deprived of dream sleep it is much harder for us to recall far events let alone those of the previous day.

REM sleep is necessary for the long-term organization of memory. If we are prevented from having enough dream sleep such data processing cannot take place. We would be unable to concentrate, find our powers of recall diminished, be irritable and, if deprived long enough, start to behave in a very bizarre manner: the system breaks down. Evans sees dreams as the essential interface between the outer world and the inner reaches of the mind.

Roxanne (16) finds that she can have a measure of control over her dreams by deliberately thinking through her day before she goes to sleep. For instance, if she watches a frightening film, she tells herself she will not dream about it and tries to deal with what has worried her about the film. Effectively she is altering the programme that her dream state needs to work on. 'By doing this,' she commented, 'I think I finish thinking about it and so tie up all the loose ends in my mind.' She does as much processing of information and feelings as she can before she sleeps, leaving her brain to work on other, hopefully less distressing, dreams. And her view is backed up by scientific research. R. Greenberg and C. Pearlman provide evidence to show that REM sleep plays an important role in assimilating information. They showed, for instance, that opportunity for REM sleep between first and second showings of emotionally disturbing films reduces emotional disturbance when the film is seen for the second time; dreams allowed the disturbing experience to be processed.

For a great number of children television and videos provide a major source of disturbing 'entertainment' during the day, and dreaming certainly is involved in the processing of the material seen. So powerful was the effect of the media on children's dreams, as they themselves recognized, that a complete chapter is devoted to it. Chapter 7 shows the profound effect that television has on the inner world of the child.

Dreaming helps us to learn

Zara (15): 'When we learn something our dreams help us to remember it.' Or to put it another way, Adam (7) delightfully and solemnly explained: 'We dream to rewind our memory.'

The REM state makes up the greater part of sleep in neonates and children when learning and personality formation is greatest. In fact, according to Greenberg and Pearlman, premature babies spend as much as 80 per cent of their total sleep time in REM sleep. This decreases with age when, says F. R. Rossi, the capacity for new learning and personality growth is reduced.

In some children the learning mechanisms have become damaged or delayed, and the effects are seen in patterns of dream sleep. For instance, when we sleep, noises around us will be interpreted by the brain and may result in an inclusion in the dream content; if it is raining on our bedroom window we might dream of a waterfall. However, autistic children do not handle incoming auditory signals in the normal way during REM sleep. Rather, they handle it in the way a new-born baby might, indicating developmental delay.

There is a lot of interesting research into the way in which chemical changes effect REM sleep patterns. Serotonin, a chemical involved in REM sleep, is found at decreased levels in certain types of mental retardation such as Down's Syndrome, so a Down's Syndrome child's REM sleep is different from that of a non-handicapped child's. Ernest Hartmann, an eminent American sleep researcher, concludes, 'Those who do not have the neuronal equipment for new learning or acquisition of information show unusually low D (Dream) time whereas those with a capacity for learning or change show high D time.'

Dreams help us solve problems

Mari (11):

> Dreaming is just like thinking in the day except no one disturbs us and we can see things more clearly because we have nothing else to think about.

This is a view that S. L. Ablon and J. E. Mach would endorse. As psychoanalysts concerned with the manifest, surface content of dreams and the latent or concealed material held within the dream, they believe dreams reflect our attempts to cope with the emotionally important material of that day or from the days just preceding the dream.

The old saying 'sleep on it' implies that while we sleep, problems are worked through and resolved. Children work through emotional difficulties and, particularly as they get older, find that dreams can actually help with practical, perhaps school-related problems. They awake to find they do know the answer to that maths problem after all. The dreaming brain has continued to process the data and has found a solution.

Dreams are a way of communicating

Celine (14) says that dreaming is important because: 'It helps us to grow up and also it tells or shows others what we are like.'

Joe (14) A wish-fulfilment dream of owning a racing car.

Dreams act as an internal information system – they are messages from ourselves to ourselves. As Lucy (12) from London noted:

> Dreams tell us what we are really like on the inside. Our subconscious is letting us know what we think.

Lucy could have been talking about Esther (11) who told me about a dream which reveals, quite directly, her inner struggles. She dreams she is a wolf, but:

> ... a witch puts me under her power and gives me to a werewolf or sometimes the prince of darkness and we go out hunting at night and by day I am a big shaggy dog so no one knows who is killing the people or animals.

I am sure that few people know that Esther is trying to sort out her confusing desires, her dark (night) and light (day) sides; her dream communicates her inner conflicts.

Another dream that Esther related makes this even more

obvious. She is concerned about changeability at that critical time when girls are changing physically and emotionally:

> The happiest dream I had was when I dreamt that some boys I know called James and Liam were trying to get me down on the ground while we were playing. I turned into a rabbit and ran away, then I turned into a horse. They laughed and jumped on my back. I turned back into a little girl and they went flying into someone's back yard.

Note how she alters. She changes from scampering rabbit to powerful horse, from being 'sat upon' to 'throwing off' her playful attackers. It is a richly symbolic dream and can be interpreted on a number of levels.

Dreams are used in various forms of therapy with children precisely because they communicate unconscious conflicts, anxieties and fears, but we will explore this in detail in Chapter 5, 'Childhood Illness and Dreams'.

Jung, master of dreams, believed that dreaming allows us to communicate not only with ourselves and others, but with the 'collective unconscious', the store of family and racial memories within our psyche. He demonstrated that not only do we dream of things which are personally important and tied in with our own experiences, but we also dream of images and symbols which are consciously completely unknown to us. Suddenly, out of the blue, we are hit by a 'big' dream that grips us. We feel it is really significant yet we do not know where it came from or why. There is a flavour of this in 15-year-old Vikki's dream:

> The happiest dream I can remember is playing in my back garden. The sun was shining and everything was peaceful . . . I saw a gate so I went through and there was a man, very old, saying, 'Go back, you've a lifetime before you come through here.'

Vikki had met an archetypal 'wise man' in her dream, someone who figures as the knowledge-giver or truth-teller in dreams across continents.

Dreams as communicators can be inspired by physical events,

like the rain described earlier, but occasionally, like Brett, you can refuse to heed a message! Brett (16) recalled that he frequently wet the bed when younger but he would dream that he was actually in the loo so it was 'alright to wee'. His view was that dreams allow you to get away with things you cannot get away with when awake. The physical pressure of his bladder was communicating to Brett that he needed to urinate. He incorporated this into his dream instead of waking up and going to the toilet.

In a sense, you could see his dream was a way of protecting his sleep; it prevented him from waking up. Freud regarded this protection of sleep as an important function of dreams. As a parent you might find it helpful to explain this idea to your child, for if she knows there are explanations for bed-wetting, she may become more relaxed and less anxious. That will help her feelings of self-esteem and, who knows, it might even reduce the bed-wetting!

Dreams as preparation

Alvin (7):

> When you want to do something you have to dream it first so you know how to do it.

This idea of dreams as a preparation for future action is not unusual. Mark dreamt he was going to stay at his friend's house a couple of days before he did so. In the dream he took his pyjama-bag to school and was picked up at the end of the day by his friend's mother. He liked the dream because he felt more confident when facing that first night away from home. The dream acted to prepare and reassure him.

Research with animals and humans shows that Mark has basically got it right. If REM sleep is interfered with, by drugs or sleep deprivation for instance, then we are less able to deal with situations for which we are unprepared. We learn from everything that happens to us during our waking lives, and through dreaming, process and store the information just in case we need it at some future point. Of course we do not 'know' what will happen to us in the future, but nature has found a brilliant way of preparing us for the unexpected.

Just prior to leaving school, many adolescents dream of what they will do when they leave. Dean (15) tells us: 'I dream about my future in general, what job I will have, where I will live, marriage and children.' He also has dreams about members of his family dying: '. . . people who I am very close to and even love I suppose. These dreams are most frightening because I know they must come true at some time.'

Dean's dreams force him to recognize his own feelings of love and to realize that he would grieve when his parents die. Typically, children and adolescents believe that their parents and loved ones will always die before them. It can be very hard to accept death, but dreams can have an important role in helping young people to come to terms with loss, as we will see in Chapter 8.

Dreams let our wishes come true

Erin (11), from Northern Ireland, sees dreams as therapeutic: 'We dream because if we have a problem then our dreams try to cheer us up.'

Dreaming adds another world to the child's waking world into which she can escape, or which allows her to experience something that is unfulfilled during the day. Erin often has happy dreams. Some of them include her grandmother whom she does not see very often. At least in the dream the wish comes true.

Escapist dreams of travel, romance, fairyland and favoured TV and pop stars delight children. In them they experience what is not available to them in waking life. Such wish-fulfilment dreams are very common in the children to whom I talked. Joe (14) from inner-city Birmingham found release from his crippling poverty, both emotional and material, in his dreams of: '. . . winning the pools, nice women, never being poor and emigrating to Australia'. Such dreams may provide satisfaction even though the dreamer believes the dream can never come true, a view put forward by Gwendolyn (15):

> I think we dream because it adds another world to our own and we need another place to escape to. Things can happen in dreams which might never happen in life but you have the experience from the dreams.

TV characters figure prominently in children's dreams, but perhaps Margaret (11) sums up romantic wish-fulfilment. She, like many girls of her age, dreams of Phillip Schofield, a very popular presenter of children's television programmes:

> I owned a frog shop and the frogs were getting on my nerves so I decided to kill them. I tried to flatten them but it did not work. I decided to send them to school late so that the teacher would beat them to death but that did not work. Then I thought I would kiss one to see what would happen and it changed into Phillip Schofield and I married him! When I told all my school friends they went to my shop and kissed all my frogs. They all turned into their favourite men and there were ten Phillip Schofields!

Catherine (13) told me that when she was younger she used to think that when she was dreaming it was really happening to a little girl in America, and during the day what happened to Catherine was really that other girl's dreams! Many adults also have commented on this aspect of dreaming. Which is the 'real' world: the one we dream of or the one we are awake in?

This may well be tied up with different levels or kinds of memory; with different parts of ourselves. We are incredibly complex beings, children and adults alike. We each have a central core but, like a diamond are many-faceted. Dreams allow us to experience aspects of ourselves that we may never have time to consider during the day.

Let us give the final explanation to Helen (13), who shows us just how knowledgeable our children can be:

> I think that while we are asleep we're still thinking and the

thoughts become animated instead of just heard. Because we are asleep we're not actually controlling our thoughts, so they become jumbled up so the characters and places change and dreams don't usually make sense. If you're thinking about something or excited, then you dream that because you're thinking about it so much. Also, if something has happened in the room while you're asleep you dream that. For instance, I was dreaming that I was carrying really heavy weights and when I woke, the cat was sitting on my back and she was heavy.

You can begin the exploration of dreams by thinking about your own and talking about them, by listening to other people's and by creating an atmosphere in which dreams are accepted and given value. In this way you set foundations for the more supportive dream-work detailed in the Chapter 3.

TWO

The Pre-School Years

New-born babies need far more REM sleep than adults. We know enough from recent research into the whole area of dreaming and its significance in early childhood development, reported by F. Crick and G. Mitchinson, to conclude that dreaming takes place in the womb, especially in the last trimester, when the foetus matures and develops highly complex processes which are essential for independent survival. It is as if REM sleep within the womb lets the baby prepare for or 'anticipate' his future world. Just as we know the foetus moves about, learns to stretch its muscles, even learns how to suck and puts that embryonic thumb into the embryonic mouth in anticipation of feeding, so REM sleep is also essential.

This large amount of REM sleep before and after birth is observed in other mammals too. It appears that REM sleep stimulates the central nervous system, which helps prepare for later structural growth. Within the uterus, scientists argue, dreaming allows the visual sensory systems to develop appropriate responses. As we humans have followed our course of evolutionary development, REM sleep has played a vital role in our survival.

According to Professor Oswald's theories, described in the last chapter, babies spend so much time in REM sleep because sleep is crucially concerned with growth and development. While slow-wave sleep, that is when we are not dreaming, helps repair the body, mental processes like memory consolidation take place during REM sleep. Other scientists believe that REM sleep provides a mechanism for the establishment of neural pathways in the brain. This goes some way to explaining why there is a change in frequency as we get older. As adults we do not need to dream as much as neonates, because those pathways have already been laid down; thus one function of REM sleep has been completed.

There is a rare condition known as Ondine's Curse in which a child is born unable to breathe and sleep at the same time. It is invariably fatal since however gently and vigilantly a mother tries to prevent her baby from sleeping she cannot do so unless a respirator is available for the baby to use. Yet the child must sleep so that the brain can do all the work we have noted so far.

REM sleep is specially important to infants, the neurologically impaired and those who have specific handicaps, such as autistic children. The brain continues to try and set down neural paths in dream sleep as a way of overcoming the handicap which inhibits effective learning. REM sleep may increase as part of the brain's attempt to cope with defects in the perceptual or motor systems. However, as we have already noted, in babies who are retarded – such as those with Down's Syndrome – there is less REM sleep.

When you watch babies sleeping, their faces seem to express all sorts of emotions from smiling amusement to disdain and annoyance. Charles Darwin thought smiling in newly born babies was an evolutionary device to ensure survival. Smiling elicits positive behaviour in the infant caretaker, so the scientists say. That certainly resonates with me. Have you ever been dragged from the depths of sleep by a crying baby only to melt to jelly (well, almost!) in response to a tender smile? Or looked at a sleeping, seemingly smiling newly born and felt totally rewarded even though you are dropping on your feet. It seems a pretty good survival tactic to me!

In infants the sleep stages overlap. They become more discreet as the brain matures, and by age 6 the transitions from stage to stage are more readily identified in EEG readings. The pattern becomes more adult-like in appearance. Unfortunately we cannot ask babies what they dream about, we can only observe and make our own guesses; but as speaking develops so toddlers can tell us about their dreams. Children of 2 do talk about dreams

Ben (5) Monsters, ghosts and giants are frequently found in the dreams of young children.

when woken during R E M sleep, as research by S. Schwartz and J. H. Johnson in American sleep laboratories reveals.

What do young toddlers dream about?

Mainly toddlers dream about family, their daily lives, and that favourite with children, animals. Because language is still fairly restricted in this age group, it is not until 3 and 4 that we begin to get a fuller picture of those 'pictures in my pillow'. Even then there are many 2- and 3-year-olds who think that dreaming happens whenever you lie in bed and close your eyes, whether or not you have fallen asleep!

At 3 years of age we often see dramatic changes in patterns of dreaming, bearing in mind that these patterns are not definitively laid down. Some 2-year-olds may be describing more sophisticated dreams while some 3-year-olds may never mention them at all. Remember, each child is unique and has its own developmental pace. Having said that, nightmares often appear at 3 years of age and, according to the thousands of dreams told to me in my research, continue to be highly represented right through to 16. It is a finding we will investigate later.

Marigold (4) attends a tiny school in a remote area. The farm on which she lives provides a lot of her dream imagery; indeed Marigold told me that her dreams come not from her head but 'from the fields' outside her window. She had a nightmare recently in which a 'biting tiger' was coming out of the cupboard in her bedroom. Like many youngsters she sometimes lies awake imagining that all sorts of dangers inhabit her room and these fears surface in dreams.

As children mature they learn to distinguish between the outside world of reality and the inner world of dreams. Up to the age of 3 children say that dreams come from God, the television or fairies. Certainly they are seen as coming from outside and as happening outside themselves, as Marigold said. This changes gradually, so that by 6 or 7 children begin to accept that dreams happen in their own heads not 'out there'.

Night terrors

Night terrors, also known as *pavor nocturnus*, are usually seen in early childhood and rarely continue beyond puberty, which may give some consolation to parents whose children suffer from them. They are caused by a dysfunction as the brain moves from one level of sleep to another. Night terrors are different from nightmares both in time of onset – usually they come in the first two hours after going to bed during non-REM sleep – and in that the child does not awaken during or immediately after the ordeal. With night terrors you may find yourself woken by a screaming, disoriented child, who is the very picture of abject terror. Although you try to reason with your wide-eyed child he may not recognize you, or he may be completely incoherent.

Other signs of night terrors are heavy breathing, distorted facial features, perspiration and moving around as if to escape whatever it is that is so terrifying. Such an episode may last ten or fifteen minutes after which time the child settles back to sleep. Usually he has completely forgotten the incident in the morning and will be surprised if told about it. However, this may not always be the case, as I have spoken to both adults and children who recall their 'night terrors'.

Although only about 3 per cent of children experience night terrors, this sleep disorder does give cause for concern. However, recent research by Bryan Lask, consultant psychiatrist of Great Ormond Street Hospital, looks particularly promising. He asked parents to observe exactly when their child had night terrors and to note what they consisted of. On the nights following the five observation sessions the parents woke the child ten to fifteen minutes before the expected terror was due. After five minutes the child was allowed to go back to sleep. This waking routine was to be stopped when the terrors ceased. Over a year after this intervention took place, there have been no relapses: the nineteen children who took part remain 'night-terror free'.

Nightmares

Nightmares usually occur in the latter part of the night during REM sleep, when all types of dreaming are most common. You can recognize nightmares by the way in which the child wakes up crying or with much upset complaining that in his 'bad dream' he has been chased, attacked or had some kind of catastrophe. With gentle reassurance and comforting the child usually returns to sleep.

Stress is a factor in causing both nightmares and night terrors. It has been suggested by I. J. Knopf that very sensitive children are more prone to nightmares, while those who suffer night terrors may have an immature nervous system. Generally nightmares and night terrors do not require medical treatment, as they usually stop spontaneously. If they happen to your child your reassurance is needed. Listen to what the child has to say, and sensitively respond to fears that are voiced. Also consider the daily events of the child; is he experiencing unusual stress at school or home? Has he had a change, such as moving house or being ill, which has upset him? Remember, children do not always speak to us of their concerns; often they communicate distress by changes in behaviour, bed-wetting, or becoming stroppy and difficult. Nightmares communicate stress too.

I experienced an example of this about six months ago. Danny, my 3½-year-old, woke up in the middle of the night crying about a bad dream. Tearfully he told me: 'A dragon was going to eat me. It lives near school. It's already eaten Desmond and Winston.' To him the dragon was as real as if it had been sitting on the end of the bed. I settled him back to sleep and, as I held his hand until he dropped off, I thought about what had been happening at his nursery.

He had been complaining that the two boys in his dream had been hitting him. There had been a number of fights, and the nursery staff were concerned that a lot of aggressive behaviour was developing with the new intake of children. Danny, who had been at the nursery for about eight months, was finding it hard to adjust to the new boys and was missing his old friends who had moved on to the infant school. He was also struggling with his own aggressive instincts and having to come to terms with wanting to hit out but being afraid of the consequences. His dream seemed to me to reflect that conflict. He managed to save himself from the dream rage by waking up, but the dragon motif continued for some time. In fact those dragons stayed around until the whole matter of his unhappiness at the nursery was resolved.

Incidently, though fairy tales are dealt with later in this book, it is worth noting that mythological themes of devouring are universal, as psychoanalysts Jung and Fordham point out.

If after trying to reassure your child you find he is still having night terrors or sleep problems over several weeks and is distressed, then do seek the advice of your doctor. Severe problems in pre-school children can be treated and you may well need to find support for yourself as well as your child. I shall explain ways you can help your child or children you work with in the next chapter.

Conflict

In the pre-school years all sorts of conflicts arise. In particular a fierce war wages between selfish, egocentric, self-satisfying inner demands and the outer demands for acceptable social behaviour. The wild child has to be tamed to fit into society, and the socialization process can be very difficult for adults and children alike.

Lucinda (12) recalled dreams of conflict she had when she was 4 years old! She would dream of shop-window mannequins with hair of different colours. Now she cannot remember what the significance of the colours was other than that red was associated with anger, while white was to do with purity, but she remembers the models with a feeling of fear. We can see how temptation here symbolizes the age-old struggle between the different parts of ourselves. We want to be both good and bad and our dreams reflect this fact:

> I used to have models from a shop window my mum used to take me to. I was only about 4 at the time when I started having them but I had them every night until I was about 8. There were two models, one with red hair the other had white hair. The red-head was evil and used to try to lead me into bad ways. The other was quiet but also bad. Different things happened every night. It doesn't sound scary but when you're 4 it is.

Animals are almost always present in the dreams of children, a finding identified in earlier research as well as more recent studies. The cats, dogs, wolves and birds that feature in these dreams very often stand in place of the dreamer. It is much 'safer' to project all our angry feelings on to a mad dream-bull for instance, than to acknowledge just how destructive we feel.

Adele (5) 'A monster is chasing a fairy.'

Such powerful emotions, all too human as they are, are covered up and often denied in 'civilized' society, and many children will be shocked and confused at their own fury. Often it is too much to take, so the dream disguises ownership and all the anger is projected on to the bull, for example.

The projection of feelings on to other characters in the dream drama, be they red-haired mannequins, hissing cats or wicked witches, is not done at a conscious level. The child has not decided to do it. Rather at a much deeper level our subconscious recognizes that emotionally we are not yet ready to face the full brunt of our own tempestuous emotions. Learning about inner drives and desires has to be paced so that we cope and learn. Too much too soon might overwhelm us.

Paula (12) was nearly overrun by early infant dreams of spiders. She told me:

> I dreamt of hundreds of tarantulas flooded round the bed. I only escaped by stepping on their heads and getting to the door.

This dream was based on a waking fear of 'creepy crawlies'. However, look at the novel way Paula finds to escape. She is not paralysed by fear but assertively finds her own strength to escape. The reaction of the dreamer in her dream is always significant, and it should never be overlooked. It tells us a lot about the inner feelings of strength or powerlessness that a child is experiencing.

Young children dream of monsters, ghosts and fairies, indeed the world of fairies is usually associated with childhood. On the one hand fairyland is a land of magic and fantasy but on the other hand it is the land of nature. Fairies live in forests and dells, in woodlands and by streams. Fairies live in a highly structured society like our own; there are kings and queens and laws which can be enforced. There are good and bad fairies, just like people. So we find children identify with fairies and dream of them.

Children watch TV and see hero/heroine characters struggling with 'baddies'. They 'recognize' the struggle between the good guy and the evil invader and they learn how hard a time characters like the three little pigs have against the greedy wolf. All this mirrors their internal struggles to be good and conform while still being sorely tempted to be naughty. I think the character Pinocchio is a lovely example of this tug of war.

Witches too symbolize the conflict between good and evil; the black-clad witch represents evil. The witch figure is an age-old stereotype devised in response to the fear of the unknown powers of the unconventional, untamed 'wise woman'. In dreams of witches, children express the stereotype found in Grimm's fairy tales, for example. The witch can be seen as a shorthand term for the cunning side of our natures, both in males and females. Witches are also used in dreams to symbolize mothers, especially if the child has just had a row with her mother and is feeling particularly angry. There are some examples of this in Chapter 8, which deals with separation and loss.

Emerging sexuality in dreams

Around 4 years old the issue of boy/girl differences comes to the fore. Lucy (12) recalled a dream she had at 4 in which 'fur was growing out of my tummy'. I wonder whether this 'fur' was in fact pubic hair? The curiosity that is prevalent at this age about bodily differences between boys and girls and adults may well show itself in dreams.

It can also be a time of difficulty getting to sleep because disturbing dreams lie in wait. Part of the difficulty may be because of the urge to masturbate. Of course such urges may occur much earlier or later, but whenever it happens, the child can feel overwhelmed and confused by the power of his or her instinctive drives. The child may be afraid of being told off. Masturbation is normal but can be problematic as Ernest Harms reveals in *Problems of Sleep and Dreams in Children*:

To go to sleep involves a transitional state where inhibitions are removed ... thus the masturbatory impulse becomes increasingly difficult to manage. At the same time this youngster may by now be plagued by disturbing dreams of nightmarish quality. If this is so he is hesitant to abandon himself to the state which allows these unpleasant occurrences to take place.

You can help by not inducing guilt in a child through making him or her feel masturbation is dirty. Children should be encouraged to understand that it is not dangerous or shameful. I have found it helpful to tell children that it is a pleasurable personal activity rather than a public event.

Obviously sexuality is a hugely important area of childhood development, but in the scope of this book I can only look at the way in which it is directly related to children's dreams. Sometimes the contents of a dream indicates sexual awareness. Aysha (4) told me about a nightmare she had in which someone put a knife in her mother when she, Aysha, was sleeping in her parents' bed. The little girl said, 'I heard some noises and I was frightened.' Was the noise in her dream or in the marital bed?

Freud's work on infant sexuality is crucial in helping us to understand how we develop as sexual beings. It does not all happen during adolescence, as we now know, but begins in infancy. Some psychologists, such as J. M. Masson, would say Freud did not go far enough; that he was scared off by the reports of incest and sexual abuse his female patients recalled from childhood and chose to see such 'incidents' as fantasy rather than as having been physically experienced. One area of children's sexual awareness was therefore hidden until the media searchlight of our own decade shocked us all by revealing just how widespread child sexual abuse is.

Freud wrote that in dreams many things are disguised so that the dreamer is not shocked into wakefulness. In fact he saw dreams as guardians of sleep. However, in terms of his theories of dreaming and sexuality he said that long thin objects, such as umbrellas and knives, were used in dreams to symbolize the penis, whereas enclosing objects such as boxes or bags, represent the vagina. Of course Aysha has never read Freud, but it is interesting to consider her dream in the light of Freudian dream theory. Maybe, half asleep, she overheard her parents having intercourse. Young children are frightened at this 'primal scene' because they don't understand it, and because love-making can appear so aggressive. Aysha's dream allowed her the opportunity to vent her fear. In my experience of working with sexually abused youngsters I have noted that when asked to draw a frightening dream, the child has often drawn herself being pursued by a man holding a knife where his penis would be.

Many of the themes pre-school children dream about are developed as they grow and mature. Let us see how these change during the next five years.

THREE

The Early School Years

Five-year-olds told me over and over again about their dreams of ghosts and monsters. In the main other subjects were witches, animals – wild, tame and mythical, immediate family and being hurt in some way. At this age there is still occasional difficulty in distinguishing between dreaming and waking reality, but largely children know that they dream, even though they may still believe the dreams come from the outside world.

Ghosts and monsters

I met Ben (6) when I went to visit some travelling families in their caravan homes. Ben shares a small caravan with his nine brothers and sisters and his mother and father. His dreams reflect his Irish origin: 'There was a Banshee on top of the roof. It flew into the room and got a girl, cut her up and made her into stew.'

Neither of Ben's parents could read or write, and most of the children had spent little time in school due to their nomadic life and because of the hostility made plain by settled communities. However, most of their traditional stories are passed on orally, and you can see that tales heard at home are highly influential:

> I dreamt of a headless man riding a horse, and once, when we pulled into a graveyard to stay the night, I dreamt of ghosts and things coming for me.

Ninety per cent of 6-year-olds in my survey dreamt about ghosts, devils and beings of that ilk. This was the peak; gradually such dreams decreased until, after another high at 11, they were hardly mentioned by 15-year-olds. Whatever the age, the feeling of being under threat from impersonal enemies is palpable, so while Saima (7) dreams of 'witches taking me away from my mum and dad', and 'white ghosts', who tell her that her mother and father are dead, Barry (13) dreamt:

> There were flashing lights outside my window and when I looked out people were running everywhere. Explosions and gun-shots everywhere. People were getting killed all over the place and when I looked closer I saw myself down there running around and hiding.

Finn (7), from a remote farming community in County Tyrone in Ireland, has the ubiquitous dreams of ghosts and laments that he has never had a happy dream, a frequent lament from children. Finn drew me a picture of an evil-looking man who was a kidnapper; he took Finn away in a bag. In Finn's drawing there is a sad-looking figure, all scrunched in a bag swung over the villain's shoulder; from the bag came a bubble of sound, plaintively saying 'help!'.

Why do children like Finn recall these distressing dreams rather than happy ones? We assume that it is because of the highly charged emotion that is attached to them. Developmental stress, unpleasant events or trauma and general everyday unhappiness are revealed in the manifest content of the dreams of ordinary children. In a way this should be no surprise as children have to undergo such major developmental changes as they mature, and the mastery of these emotional and physical changes is the work of childhood. Dreams often communicate just how difficult such work is, a fact we adults all too frequently overlook.

These threatening dream characters over time change from monsters and ghosts to anonymous males and impersonal enemies, or worse, known members of the family. C. W. Kimmins, a London inspector of schools, collected a vast number of dream narratives from children in 1918 and it is interesting to compare today's findings with those of seventy years ago. He discovered that 25 per cent of the frightening dreams of children under 8 consisted '... chiefly of the dread of objectionable men'. Otherwise, apart from dreams of air-raids, children today dream of the same subjects.

Nightmares

Between the ages of 5 and 11 most children experience troublesome nightmares at some time, and though they may include the ubiquitous ghost we have already mentioned, the content varies. Nightmares are upsetting for children and parents alike because they elicit such unhappy and frightened feelings in the child, feelings which may linger for days. In a study by American Louise Bates Ames it was found that half of the children suffered from nightmares. My figure is higher: overall I found that 63 per cent of children who took part in the survey had nightmares; in Northern Ireland the figure was 71 per cent.

Animals often symbolize threatening forces in the dreams of children. They may represent archetypal elements in the Jungian sense in that they are not based on personal experience, but stem from our common human heritage, our collective unconscious memory of the past. There was a time in our evolutionary history when animals and insects were daily enemies, and for young children fear of raw animal potency is very obvious in dreams.

Christopher (6) dreamt of a ferocious giant two-headed caterpillar which squashed his house and then ate him. Dreams affected his waking behaviour. For instance, he dreamt that there was a monster in his mother's bag and next day would not go near it, skirting round his mother when out shopping, just to avoid contact! The line between dreams and reality is still very thin at this stage of a child's development.

Helen (13):

When I was about 5 I dreamt that my school friends and I were being chased by wolves and when they caught us they would eat us.

Helen's dream may have been triggered by the story of the

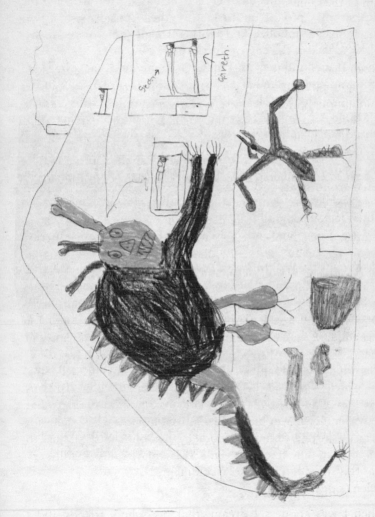

Gareth (7) 'I am sometimes frightened when my dog opens my bedroom door, then when I sleep I dream of monsters breaking in to attack my family.'

Three Little Pigs of course, and it's always useful when trying to understand dreams to consider simpler explanations rather than complex ones. Look for 'day debris', such as stories surfacing in dreams. If that proves unsatisfactory then consider what the dream animals symbolize and work through some of the techniques described at the end of the chapter.

When I was talking to Linda (10) she told me about a recurring nightmare she has had since she was 5 years old. In it, she said, '. . . there is a man, a devil, taking me away. Then there are people coming after me trying to kill me'. Dreams she has now are also quite terrifying:

> There is me and a lady. I was crying. Catapulted into a lady's garden. Then I'm being chased by a man. He chopped me up.

She sleep-walks, and was once nearly killed after walking out of the house late one night.

I did not probe into Linda's dreams, apart from gently remarking that such dreams must be upsetting for her. She volunteered that it was all because of 'a big secret' that happened when she was 5. Her best friend Lucy, who was close by Linda all this time, offering shy, smiling encouragement, knew all about it and the teacher did too; that was where I left it with Linda. I discovered that a man had been imprisoned because of gross offences against the child. What is so striking for me is that Linda is still obviously unable single-handedly to come to terms with her dreadful experiences. Her dreams communicate that her very deep-seated fears have yet to be worked through. Professional help can be obtained through specialist agencies such as the school psychological service or the NSPCC, who have workers trained in counselling victims of sexual abuse.

Post-traumatic nightmares

The kind of nightmare that Linda experiences is a special type of recurring, often literal, nightmare that follows overwhelmingly intense and unexpected outside events. They may continue for years but particularly at times when the dreamer is reminded of her past helplessness. Lenore Terr, a member of staff at the University of California School of Medicine, studied a group of twenty-six children who had been kidnapped from their school bus in Chowchilla, California, and then buried alive by their three abductors. They were held captive for about twenty-seven hours. A year after their ordeal and four to five years later the children, whose ages ranged from 5 to 14 years, still had nightmares which exactly repeated the trauma and, additionally, many of the group tended to walk, talk or scream in their sleep.

As time passed the Chowchilla children tended to elaborate the recurrent dreams of the kidnapping so that in some cases the original trauma became hidden underneath other material. However, such disguised nightmares still tell us that traumatic experiences deeply affect children's psyches and they need help to exorcise the pain. Other children who have had a psychologically overwhelming life event dream that they themselves die. Terr points out that personal-death dreams and recurrent nightmares often indicate that a traumatic event has taken place in the past, and these children allow themselves to die in their dreams because they no longer believe in personal invulnerability.

Family dynamics

Families can be warm and loving, cruel and destructive, a mixture of all of these or just 'good enough' – good enough to nourish the offspring so that there is an adequate sense of self-worth and confidence in order for the child to make her way in the world. Families can be hard to survive, as Robin Skynner and John Cleese show in *Families and How To Survive Them*. For most children, however, the family is where we start from, where we begin to have a sense of who we are. In receiving thousands of dream narratives from children the importance of the secure caring unit, be it single parent or wide, extended family, becomes more and more apparent. We can see from the following dreams how the child's perception of family dynamics is communicated through dreams.

Giorgio (5), after his parents had been cross with him, dreamt: '. . . they turned into baddies and tried to get me. I was frightened. All the family changed into baddies except me.' In the dreams he sees their faults, for they are 'the baddies' while he is good. He expresses his fear of anger when expressed by his family. Bob (7), whose parents recently split up, has wishfulfilment dreams in which an anonymous professor builds a space ship that takes the boy to China where his father is waiting. Absent parents frequently figure in the dreams of children whose parents, or parental figures, have separated.

Chandra (7), who has a baby brother as well as a little sister, had a nightmare which made her cry:

A baby monster took my baby away to his castle. The monster's mum came and took my baby away and I never saw my baby, ever.

Many young children call their baby brother or sister 'my baby', as Chandra does. Possessiveness, affection and a sense of responsibility towards the younger sibling mix together. Sometimes that feeling of responsibility can become guilt-inducing, as we will see in the dreams of older children.

Cheryl (7) has had disturbing dreams about her aunt's baby being hurt in a fall and she feels in some way guilty. But then many of her dreams show fear of one sort or another. She dreams that her mother runs away, leaving her father to take care of the family; and, when ill, images of a needle that sucks out all her blood invade her sleeping hours. When asked why we dream, Cheryl replied, 'Because we're frightened.' This vivid image of being drained – of blood – tells us that Cheryl feels exhausted by the demands her world is making on her. She needs someone to help her build up her physical and emotional energy, otherwise she will be sucked dry.

Powerlessness

Children wrestle with feelings of powerlessness and seek means of survival. Claudette (6) is ultimately successful in her dream struggle but it involves enormous effort to be so.

I dream about my sister. It is a terrible dream. Leeanne sat on the chair near the window, she's like at the pictures. Someone was near the window. It was a ghost. He strangle her. She was flat dead on the floor, but he was still strangle her. I was near and asleep. I woke up and saw her on the floor. I woke up crying but she was in her bed.

She wrote of another dream in which her sister again features centrally:

I dream about the devil. We all went down to the devil. He wouldn't let us go so he said, dig in the garden. I was sweating, then we found a knife. We sneaked in the house and stabbed the devil and we went back up, they were glad.

In some families where there is a great deal of upset, brothers and sisters dream of helping each other and of sticking together against the world. Claudette's sister is her lifeline, her closest loved person, so her dream tells us of her extreme anxiety about her sister being hurt. In the final dream, together they overcome the life-threatening evil but they have to go down to the depths to do so. In Jungian terms they seek a solution in the dark world of emotion. It would be of little use for Claudette to seek a solution in her head – in the attic as it is often symbolized in dreams – because it is gut instinct for survival and her animal sweat which will get her through.

Such assertive action is unusual at Claudette's age Ames explains:

It is interesting that though fear dreams are extremely prominent, especially up through 7 years, there is a definite lack of aggressive dreams in which the child is angry or in which he attacks others. Though the child is implicitly an important figure in the dream at all ages, it is not until 7 that he seems to become the central acting figure, and not just the recipient of some activity (i.e. earlier he is chased). This coincides with the trend in fears. In fears, the child begins to fear things especially about himself around 7 years of age. Earlier he feared that his mother would be separated from him, and fears of that sort, but at 7, fears and worries are real personal fears about himself. In tracing the development of the sense of self, we find this reasonable, since 6 is an age of marked increase in separation of the self from the mother, and 7 is the age when the child is consolidating his own sense of self.

Children spoke with relentless monotony of television- and video-inspired dreams. In some cases it was obviously reflected cartoon characters and children's stories but all too often it was material meant for adults. Phillip (6) described watching *The Little House of Horrors* and *The Fly*, both viewing for adults. He now has bloody nightmares of a man who zips his head off. Josie (7) also has horror video-instigated dreams, with the added dimension that her mother, father and brother, whom she watches with, turn into attacking monsters as well. They are certainly not doing anything to protect her from the violence. The impact of such a televised diet is covered in detail in Chapter 7.

Anxiety dreams

When I was in one school interviewing children, a teacher took me to one side to ask me about her daughter's dreams. It seemed that her 6-year-old, Alana, was regularly having disturbing dreams, so much so that it was difficult to get her to bed at night; she was frightened that those horrible dreams would come again. We talked about ways in which they could deal with such dreams, talk about them, draw them, or act them out, as described in detail at the end of this chapter. I gave the teacher a questionnaire for Alana to complete with her mother's help to see if that threw further light on the cause of these unpleasant dreams. The speedy reply contained the comment, 'Alana was very keen to talk about her dreams and happily went to sleep tonight! Perhaps I should have discussed them with her more often.'

Alana's dreams of being chased by men, and also of dragons and spiders, are typical dreams for this age. But, in addition, many of her dreams concerned being shouted at by 'wicked ladies' with angry faces. These are linked with school 'where you have a not very nice time'. Other dreams involved her mother running off or not being available to protect Alana from those who shout at her or who are in some other way uncaring. It transpired that school and 'dinner ladies' were at the root of her anxiety. If you listen to your children talk about dreams you may well discover what their anxieties are.

In 'chase' dreams at this age the pursuer may be an inanimate object. Sally (13) was 6 when she dreamt about a washing machine that chased her around the room. Then she dreamt about a malevolent toilet:

> I used to dream about toilets opening and closing and eating people up whenever they used them. I dreamt that they filled up with water when someone shuts the door after they've used it. I dreamt that I'd used it, went out and remembered that I'd left something in there and went back. The door slammed I couldn't get out and I drowned.

It is easy to lose sight of the fact that things we take for granted, like toilets and washing machines, can be seen as noisy, frightening presences which have a life of their own.

Wish-fulfilment and adventure

Wish-fulfilment dreams play a significant role in young children's dreams. They dream of having presents, lovely rainbows, toys, sweets and friends, though too many children said they had never had a happy dream, ever! In 1918–19, according to C. W. Kimmins, the Chief Inspector of London schools who carried out a survey of children's dreams, wish-fulfilment dreams were the same then as they are now, except in one area: then girls particularly dreamt of the return of fathers and brothers from the war.

Some children leap off into highly imaginative worlds. Sohail (7) dreams of being turned into a robot, being a white car that can speak, making inventions and having wings so that he can fly to Hollywood to meet his favourite TV stars! Kyla (7) has a most frightening dream: 'Margaret Thatcher is cutting off my nose.' While Danielle (7) had a happy dream in which she was walking on the waves of an ocean, then living in the water and blowing bubbles like a fish.

Dreams of bravery and adventure are not found too often in this age group. Keziah (6) was a rare example, for she has a particularly empowering dream. In it, she says:

> I can change into anything I want and do anything. I changed into the strongest person in the world and I went to help people in fires.

And Kimmins tells us that in 1918 a 7-year-old boy dreamt:

> I was an American soldier, and I had an army of soldiers and we went into Germany and we captured the Kaiser and Little Willie.

Parents find ways of helping with children's bad dreams, as Zara and Delores relate. Zara (15) remembered that when she was about 6 she had a dream in which 'bad penguins' came into her room. Her mother had to come in and 'kill' them all before Zara could go back to sleep. Delores (5) told me that she has nasty dreams about monsters and ghosts and other frightening things that want to attack her, but she's now found some comfort for, 'I tell my mum or now, I pray. That helps.' We work through other ways to help later in the chapter.

Differences in age and sex

There are differences in dreams according to the child's sex as well as age. David Foulkes's longitudinal research into this, that is research on the same group of people over a period of years, shows no significant differences in the dreams of pre-school boys and girls; animals and monsters are themes common to both. However, there comes a marked sex-difference in dream content at ages 5 to 6. Then, Foulkes finds, boys' dreams are more likely to be centred on conflict, often with male strangers or untamed animals, whereas girls are engaged in more friendly dream relationships. As the years pass, similarities and differences continue to emerge in their dreams. These reflect the way in which boys and girls experience and view the world differently and the variety of socialization processes that act upon each gender to reinforce the stereotyped image of male and female.

Between ages 8 and 10 many children like to talk about dreams, and if wakened in the middle of one try to go back and finish it. They talk to mothers rather than fathers about their dreams as mothers are usually more willing to listen without being dismissive. By about 13 though, friends are more often chosen as the audience. The dreamer is generally the central actor of the dream, while friends and family continue to play major roles. Wish-fulfilment dreams continue but become more tied to social goals, as Amir's (8) dream shows. He dreams he can speak good English and can play football. If he could do these things in his waking life, he believes the other boys at school would accept him.

Alicia (8) has pleasurable fairy-tale dreams of princes and kings and queens. Indeed, she was quite unusual in that she could not recall ever having a nightmare. This optimism is to be seen in the reason she gave for dreaming. She said, 'We dream to make people loving and kind.' In other dreams told to me children have found themselves rescued from danger by parents or kind relatives, reflecting their sense of trust in these adults. Life has not been so kind to Bridgit.

Dealing with trauma

An intelligent articulate girl from Dublin, Bridgit (8) has experienced a number of tragedies. Her family friend, a woman 'who had been sad for a long time', hanged herself. Bridgit's family, hard pressed to make ends meet, moved to England, where she started at a new school. All these major life changes, life 'stressors', happened within the last four months. Her dreams reflect these traumas. Though her happiest dreams are about having nice clothes and being rich in a fairy tale sort of way, the painful dreams are of a much darker hue:

A nightmare about a man up in the sky with a dog with two heads on it. Mammy went out but she did not think the dog was alive. It was making her bleed. Mammy got a stick and broke it. The man up in the sky was happy. At the last bit, Mammy died ... I dream of Maureen that died. She is shouting 'I will get her' and has weapons to hurt me.

Bridgit drew her dead friend lifting a sword and swinging a mace in the air ready to smash them down on the terrified child. In a way her friend has already dealt the blow, for the knowledge that her friend took her own life is a dreadful truth for Maria to contemplate. If adults on whom children rely, adults to whom they give love, act in such a way, how can children comprehend the world? The girl still seemed shell-shocked.

I was not able to work through this material with Bridgit. However, I was able to spend a little time with her talking about separation and loss, for she had lost her friend, her old school, her home and her country. She was one of so many children struggling with tremendously powerful life events. There is much archetypal material in her dream. The two-headed dog, like Janus the 'January' god, who sees the old and the new, the past and future. Dogs in ancient mythology were the companions of the dead on their 'night sea-crossing' from the world of the living to the world of the dead. In symbolic terms the mace, a very unusual item to see in the dream of an 8-year-old, denotes a crushing blow or utter destruction, the annihilation of the assertive tendency in mankind, not merely victory over a foe. The intensity of this archetypal imagery tells us how grave an effect Bridgit's circumstances have had on her psyche. The indifference of the callous 'man-in-the-sky' god reveals a fear that there is not even a higher being who will give support.

Kidnap

Feelings of being unprotected are revealed in dreams of being kidnapped, a very prevalent theme in the 6- to 10-year-old group. Cassandra (7):

The most frightening dream I've had was when I got kidnapped by two men and they drove me away to a forest and kept me there for a week.

Umza (9):

The frightening dream I have had is about my sister on her tricycle riding on to the road and someone sees her and takes her away and I can't stop thinking about that.

In some cases the child changes from victim to rescuer and asserts personal power. Hamish (8) dreamt about men with guns tying him and his brother up and then kidnapping them. Though they managed to escape, it is interesting that Hamish also rescued his mother and father as well as his brother. A healthy hero instinct is disclosed, for his other dreams are about being a successful detective, being 'a good army man' and being a great sportsman. Oonagh (10), from a farming community in Northern Ireland, had dreams in which she was taken away from her family:

I was riding my bike and a dog came after me. Then a kind of green ghostly man jumped out and put me in a deep sleep, brought me to his cave and threw me in a dog's den. Then I woke up and thought there was a dog in my room.

While she was powerless against the 'green man', a traditional wild man figure in folklore throughout the world, in other circumstances she is more than capable. Another time she dreamt of finding a bomb outside her house and being the only one able to defuse it. Oonagh gives voice to a waking wish shared by many living in our war-torn world.

In Kimmins's study, which I mentioned earlier, carried out seventy years ago, I could find no references to dreams of being kidnapped recorded for this age group. There are so many similar themes in other areas, yet children then did not report fear dreams of kidnapping. How is this explained? Is it a reflection of our society in which children feel unprotected? Is it that the influence of media and its content, ensures that few

Oonagh (10) Fears of being chased by strangers provide distressed cries of 'Help' in many children's dreams.

children feel completely safe? Whatever the causes, these dreams tell us in no uncertain terms that our children do not feel safe.

Dream houses

When I was researching my book *Women Dreaming* I soon realized that in the majority of women's dreams the recurring image of the house symbolized the person's sense of themselves. Different levels of the house may be used to represent distinctive psychological aspects. So the attic may symbolize the thinking processes, being in our 'heads'; the cellars may signify being in touch with our unconscious, dark hidden drives, and so on. When I came across Helen's (13) dream, which she had at 9 years of age, it became obvious that this can be a potent symbol early in our lives. Helen dreamt:

> The house fell down. It fell down in stages. First the front, then the back, then the middle. My father, sister and I were all in the house but my mum was out at work. We were trying to burrow under the floor to get out of the way of falling bricks, and all I could think about was what mum would think when she got in.

On a very simple level Helen might be worried about her mother's reaction when she comes home from work and finds the house a shambles. Many of us are not at our best after finishing a day's work. Tired, we get back to a mess and start to complain to those children, partners or whoever, who have been in the house and done nothing! So Helen's dream may be dramatically depicting that scenario. However, it may reveal that Helen feels her defences, as symbolized by the protective structure of the house, are falling apart. Her father and sister are affected by this also and equally trying to avoid the danger, but they need to go deeper in order to escape. What does Helen's family have to dig/delve into to resolve the situation?

Anger

Diane's mother, a single parent, is very busy doing a university course in Edinburgh. Every evening she studies so the television cannot be switched on as the noise would disturb her. Diane is expected to be quiet and amuse herself. At the weekends she goes to stay with her grandparents, or other relatives, so she has very little time with her mother. There is a strong bond between the two and Diane (9) obviously loves her mother very much, but part of her is angry, as these dreams reveal:

> Happiest dream was when I was in the Land of Nod and everyone was being really, really kind to me and being a servant for me.

While her most frightening one was: 'When my teddies came alive and killed my mum.'

Why doesn't mummy spend more time with me? Why does mummy love her books more than me? Those are the questions that Diane asks herself. She feels upset and this shows in the killing of her mother in the dream. Of course, it isn't Diane that would do such a thing, it is those bad teddies, but symbolically the teddies give vent to her hostile feelings.

Fear

Douglas (9), from Essex, dreamt about the ozone layer breaking up and the heat on earth becoming unbearable. He also frequently has dreams about nuclear war and these scare him a great deal. He suggested that 'children just learn these adult problems and think "it's not very nice" and then dream about them'. Both boys and girls dreamt of danger from outside forces such as fire, and these dreams seem to increase after the age of 8. Chantelle (9) has an amalgamation of fears: being shot in the back, her family being imprisoned in a dungeon and the shadows in her room. In her happiest dream she finds a way to erase all this fear by, 'Killing the devil and making things better for the world and for me.'

At 10 years of age nightmares still predominate over good dreams, and though some children may cry out, most do not wake up. There are still wish-fulfilment dreams, like Perihan's (9) happiest dream in which she turned into a princess and could have everything in the world that she wanted. However, in her regular nightmare, she said:

> I was in bed and there was a spider in the corner of the bedroom and it grew and grew and actually tried to eat me up.

Waking moods are often coloured by the dreams we have. Emma (10) gives us a fine example of this:

> Once when I was sick I dreamt that my sister was Dracula and for weeks after that I refused to sleep in the room with her. She teased me by showing her teeth.

Children's dreams reflect daytime events, as we have already seen. What goes on in the village, community or world affects our dreams. Surprisingly, school features very little but other areas certainly make up for that lack. Dreams prompted by fear of the dark end up with the dreamer being locked in unlit rooms with unidentifiable monsters. Neil (10), from a farming community, dreams about falling in a slurry pit. Obviously, waking warnings of the dangers are being dramatized in his dreams.

Inner-city dweller Nigel (10) dreams of being beaten up, someone coming upstairs to get him, and monsters. He said, quite candidly, 'If I watch scary videos, I have nightmares.' He also, occasionally now, has dreams of riding his bike and being

Alicia (8) 'I dream that I am magic and doing magic tricks at a show.'

knocked off it again. Two years ago he was hit by a car while out in the street riding and he was in hospital for some time with a broken leg. In his dreams he relives the trauma as his mind tries to find a way of making sense of the experience. Until Nigel comes to terms with the shock, his accident-dream will probably continue. If he can talk through the feelings he had at the time of the accident, his fears and even maybe his guilt at being in some way to blame, then the dream will probably go away. Until the trauma is exorcized the dream will keep nudging him to finish off the 'unfinished business'.

Sibling rivalry

Often children resent their brothers and sisters. This sibling rivalry, though very trying, is normal, and many psychologists would argue that it is a very necessary preparation for mixing with other people outside the family. In many instances negative feeling about siblings are given expression in dreams. Gideon (10):

> I dreamt our house was bombed and that we ran away and hid. Then loads of soldiers came into the house looking for us. We discovered we'd left my older brother behind, then I woke up!

On one level he certainly would like to leave his brother behind, but pressure from family and society ensures that he does not voice such a wish too loudly. Cassandra (7) dreamt that her brother got a really good toy but she broke it. She feels like doing that in waking life sometimes but dare not. In her dream she can get away with it! Similarly Sinead (8) dreams that her elder brother, whom she says she hates, was killed by a bomb when he went away on an army posting and she was relieved to hear the news. In another of her dreams he turned into a dog. No love lost there!

Happiness is . . .

Soap operas, such as *Neighbours*, influence many childhood dreams, as Candice (9) knows. In her dream:

I went to a concert to see Kylie Minogue. Then we met outside after it finished. And we were friends.

Otherwise happy dreams may be about being bridesmaids, having lovely food and sweets, going to parties and playing. As Dana tells us: 'I got the bouncing castle to my house and I could jump from my bedroom window all day long.'

Holidays are also pleasurable dream themes. The happiest holiday-dreams of 10-year-old Missy are set in Ireland. In them she goes to stay with her grandmother and has a wonderful time, cosseted and petted, in a 'lovely wee house'.

Missy leads the traveller's life in the family's gleaming chrome-and-blue trailer, with its shining etched-glass windows and spotless lace-covered interior. When I visited her I picked my way across the squalor of the tyre-strewn, litter-covered unofficial site, which also boasted dead rats lying in oil-rainbowed puddles. Her family were doing well and they had just bought an equally spotless, smaller trailer, which was used as a bedroom for the four older children, while mother and father slept with the two youngest children in the chrome beauty. But the new arrangement had a major drawback for Missy; before, when she had nightmares, often horror-film triggered, she could dive into 'mum and da's bed'. Now, instead of that physical reassurance and comforting, her sisters have to console her.

Helping children with their dreams

How do you console your child? Whether you are a caring parent whose child has a bad dream or a person who works with children as a nurse, teacher, childminder or youth worker, there are times when you will want to actively 'do something' to help. Although there are an enormous variety of dreams, only a few simple techniques are needed to work with them. Should you try these and problems with dreams do not diminish, then seek professional help.

1 Try to create a caring, accepting, non-judgemental atmosphere. Dreams are not 'right' or 'wrong' so you must not tell a child that they are bad, silly or horrible to have dreamt whatever they have dreamt about.

2 Respect the child's need for confidentiality. If she chooses to talk to other people about her dreams, fine, but do not abuse the trust she has put in you by talking to others without permission.

3 Listen to what the child says and ask open questions that encourage her to explore the dream. For example: 'How did you feel in the dream?' 'Did you find anyone to help you when you were being chased?' 'What was the nicest part of the fairyland place you went to?' By listening you show the child that you value what she has to say and this increases the child's self-esteem and trust in you. Dreams cannot be worked on unless there is trust between the dream teller and the dream hearer; this alliance is a vital part of the process.

4 Allow the child to express her feelings about the dream and go at her own pace. Do not force a child to go on talking about dreams when she wants to stop. Respect the child's right to privacy, remembering that you are not a psy-

choanalyst, but a supportive adult in a non-clinical setting. Most children need a grown-up friend, not a therapist.

5 Help the child make links to events in waking life. If a child has an upsetting dream gently try to find out if there is anything upsetting her in waking life. Children can become much more aware of internal psychic pressures by working on dreams. Carl's dream described below gives an example of this developing self-awareness.

6 Some children believe that if they talk about a dream it will come true. Help educate children about dreams so that they understand the purpose of dreaming.

7 If the child wants to, and it seems appropriate, encourage more active ways of working on dreams:
a. Draw the dream. Look at it. Talk about it. Ask the child if she would like to change it and if so how? She might want her dog to come and be with her, so draw in her dog. She might want the offending monster to be destroyed so paint over it or cut it out. The aim is to generate positive responses to dealing with whatever has caused the distress.
b. Act out the dream. If the child has been chased in the dream, she may, with your help, feel secure enough to re-enact the dream. You might have to play a chasing monster, but before you start plan a way for the child to deal successfully with the threat. Maybe she can make friends with it, maybe she wants to destroy it; perhaps she could talk to it and tell it to stop being so horrible. The aim is to enable the child to confront the danger and, with your support, to find a way of dealing with that dream situation.

Carl (9) has temper tantrums in which he directs much of his anger against his mother. One evening, after a particularly aggressive outburst, his mother sent him to bed. That night Carl had a nightmare:

. . . there was an eye running about and a devil killed me, but I came back alive and killed my mum because the devil was controlling me.

He woke up with a pencil in his hand, held like a dagger.

This sort of dream, though distressing, allows the child to express the anger and frustration felt during waking hours. The highly dramatized dream drama enabled Carl also to deny his responsibility, since it is the devil in the dream who is 'controlling' him. We all find it difficult to accept the intense negative emotions that we feel, and Carl is no different to many adults and children. He does not really want to own the 'bad' part of himself.

So, what can we do to help youngsters like Carl grow through such feelings? One thing is to talk about the dream and talk about the feelings, reassuring him that all of us have 'good' and 'bad' feelings, that we all at times want to hit back at people who we think have hurt us and let us down. Explain that part of growing up is learning to control the impulses to attack others. Dreams let us express those hostile feelings without physically hurting the person they are aimed at. Carl can get his own back on his mother but still wake up caring for her – and with a sense of relief that she is unharmed!

Such violent dreams are not particularly unusual, especially where there are a lot of conflicts in a very close relationship, whether they be through outside pressures, such as unemployment, or through family dynamics. Whatever the cause, such dreams can act as a catharsis and a starting point for talking through unresolved feelings of distress and unhappiness. Carl said he does talk to his mother about his dreams, so they would be an ideal vehicle for them to talk about the difficulties in their life together. He also needs to be reassured that he is not 'mad' or going to be a wicked criminal because he has these dreams. He needs to know that almost all children and adults have disturbing dreams about which they feel anxious or ashamed.

Marie (8) had a particularly traumatic time when her brother suffered a deep head wound. She regularly dreams that this happens again and, most terrifyingly, that it is her father who hit him in the first place. In other dreams she and her brother are locked up by a man who is jealous of them and he is going to kill them. Her happiest dream? 'I saved someone because I was changed into a Supergirl.' This 8-year-old has to become like Wonder-Woman in order to protect others! But who is protecting her?

Her dreams certainly indicate that no obvious person fulfils that role. Indeed, Marie hoped that my book might help children to forget about their dreams because all dreams do is scare her. What I hope my book will do is not help children to 'forget' dreams such as these, but push parents and others who care for and work with children to realize that children's deepest fears and anxieties signal to us through dreams. We as responsible caring adults can help them work through the pain and terror. We ought to be able to help if necessary. We ought to be able at least to listen to some of the burdened outpourings of children. We ought to show them we care enough to listen without ridiculing or passing judgement. If we do that we can enable trust to flourish, and that for some children may be the first time that they have been able to put trust in an adult without that trust being abused.

Gideon (10) recalled a recurring dream in which he was inescapably entwined in a massive black metallic structure. He said, looking back, that it represented his life at that age. This imagery of being enclosed, trapped, held in impersonal surroundings and being powerless, figure in many children's dreams. You can help a child to make links with waking circumstances. Where does he feel trapped and why? You may be able to highlight an escape route that he has not noticed.

Bruce (8) has dreams of being in space. He dreams of his father who died 'a long time ago'. But the dreams don't serve to comfort him; they make him sad. He talks to his brother about his dreams but his mother does not spend the time to listen to them. But then, he would not talk about his 'dad' because no one ever mentions him at home – his mother doesn't like it. Bruce has never been allowed to grieve.

Sometimes in Bruce's dreams, aliens from space come down and eat him up. I told Bruce that I would find that a frightening dream; I empathized with his discomfort. He moved on to tell me that his happiest dream was having a holiday and not going to school. I asked him how he felt about school. His reply about constant 'battering' and his timid demeanour prompted me to explore a little further. Did he ever tell the teachers about being bullied? 'No, I don't tell anyone.'

Can Bruce ever get maximum benefit from school if he is beset by such worries? The devouring aliens symbolize the boys who bully him at school. They are 'alien' to him. Their boisterous extroversion is the antipathy of his bowed reticence. There is no one, at school or at home, to whom Bruce can talk because he believes no one wants to listen.

If you want to help a child like Bruce, listen: it is one of the most valuable helping skills there is.

FOUR

The Later School Years

In Great Britain most children change school at 11. They transfer from the small world of the primary school, where they are in contact with a limited number of teachers, to the larger secondary school where subject-ridden timetables cause them to move from room to room, teacher to teacher, throughout the day. Obviously this has a detrimental effect on many youngsters. Coupled with rapidly changing physical characteristics and hormonal changes, it is not surprising to see many dreams of insecurity at this time.

School

Though dreams about school are generally not prevalent in childhood, at this transition stage and at times of examinations they become much more apparent. Louise (11), an artistic girl from Shropshire, had a terrifying dream about school:

> The dream which is the most terrifying I have ever had is, me and my brother went to this science lesson and we sat down, and when my brother got something wrong, the teacher pulled this lever and he fell down a trap door and fell on to this thick knife, and it went through his stomach.

Two things here: Louise is not looking forward to leaving her present cosy country school and the teachers she is so fond of, and she is fearful of the new, large secondary school she must attend. She has been the subject of older pupils' mythology-mixed-with-truth tales in which the 'new kid' is subject to horror stories guaranteed to scare. Louise needs assurance about her new school; an organized visit with a chance to meet the teachers may well stop her fears flourishing. She also worries about anything happening to anyone in her close-knit family. Talking through these anxieties would help.

Helen (13) has distressing dreams about setting off for school in her school uniform only to find, along the way, that in its place are her ordinary clothes. She is frustrated when she tries to go back home and change as something always prevents her. Typically Helen is afraid that the teachers will shout at her.

Clothes often represent the way in which we present ourselves to the world – a persona that we put on according to what we want people to see. School uniforms signify adherence to an imposed school code or discipline. They are the source of regular friction between pupils and teachers as children seek to establish individuality rather than conform to imposed uniformity. Helen, who is academically successful and popular at school, would like to rebel a little, to assert her independence, but the dream indicates that she fears the disapproval that would ensue.

Roxanne (16) was in the throes of examinations when she had the following dream. Her successful performance in the rite-of-passage that examinations are in western society was central to her future plans, so she dreamt of struggling to reach the 'heights':

> I am frightened of heights and dreamt that I was hanging by my fingertips from a window-sill on the top floor of our school. I was trying to pull myself up and climb into the window so I could get to a lesson I was late for.

She has to hold on that 'top floor' level. Symbolically she has reached high and, though she has some doubts about her abilities to keep it up, she is determined to get to her goal.

Fear of not achieving well in school, being suspected of lying, poor school reports and being sent to the headteacher, all figured highly in children's rating of stressful life events in a cross-cultural study of children from six countries published in the journal *Child Psychology and Psychiatry*. They felt acutely the humiliation meted out by sarcastic teachers. What the children said they felt was often different from what adults around perceived, indicating that we must listen to what children tell us rather than assume we know how they feel. We need to try to understand the structure and function of childhood from the inside and one way is to attend to what children communicate through dreams.

The wider world affects school life and details are regularly included in dreams. Kimberley (11) relates:

> I was in my classroom alone, nobody was there. I heard a helicopter flying around outside, then it dropped a pink-wrapped present with a purple-and-yellow bow. I picked up the present and untied it and bang! Then the whole school blows up and I die and go to hell!

At some level Kimberley recognizes that she is in an explosive situation, as she is in her Belfast home, where helicopters do patrol day and night. However, it may well relate to another situation which on the surface is quite pleasant and nicely wrapped up, but blows up in her face. When you meet a dream like this consider what is likely to be happening to the child which could cause such an expectation.

Taking responsibility

Around the age of puberty home remains a significant setting in girls' but not boys' dreams. Janice (12), who lives in a small village in County Tyrone, has happy dreams about being on holiday in a sunny place and about eating loads of sweets, but she has a number of dreams that involve her taking responsibility for her mother in some way:

> I dream about being in the devil's house doing puzzles to keep my mum alive and I always try to change the dream into something nice because it is horrible.

Many ancient myths and legends involve puzzles and riddles which the hero/heroine has to solve. Such tests put an awesome burden on the puzzler and a high price for failure, as is the case in Janice's dreams.

Janice also dreams that her mother falls off a bridge, and she has to dive in to the river to save her, this again is a recurring dream. Such dreams cause her to call out for her mother who immediately comes and comforts her. At a deep, unconscious level she seems terribly afraid of anything happening to her mother and is prompted constantly to seek assurances that she is alright. The initiation of the process of separation which is an important part of adolescence is proving hard for Janice.

Emma (10), who lives with her mother and three sisters, has many nightmares. In this one she goes to the rescue:

> I had a nightmare of my sister falling off a high cliff and I jumped after her but at the bottom of the cliff a man walked to where my sister was going to fall and just caught her and I felt myself bang on the floor and woke up.

Fortunately there is an adult figure who can successfully intervene where her efforts fail. The sensation of falling out of bed is incorporated into the dream here. This is not at all unusual as we noted earlier.

Being left behind

Many children in this age group dream of literally being left on their own, as Nasreen (11) does.

> I once dreamed about my brother drowning in the shower, because I told him not to play with water, he disobeyed me and died. After that I dreamt about all my family walking to London airport to go to India. I was too slow and lost my way.

Rosaleen (11), described her most frightening dream:

> I dreamt about going home but my brother runs away from me, and when I get home none of my family knows me and I travel around, nowhere to go. So, I go to my friend's house but they think I am a stranger and close the door in my face.

The price Nasreen and Rosaleen pay for not being able to take on the adult role is the loss of a brother and the desertion of a family. Guilty feelings about inability to care adequately for others are found particularly in the dreams of girls. Again and again, it would appear, girls are being pushed into taking responsibility for others at too young an age and at the expense of their own childhood freedom. The ultimate cost may be that girls become women trapped in the role of taking care of their partner's needs, even when it harms themselves. Robin Norwood graphically describes this in *Women Who Love Too Much*.

Dreams where everyone else has died and the dreamer is the only person left alive are common around puberty. In some cases the family leaves, while in others tragedy strikes, such as all the dreamer's family being killed in a car crash so he is left to fend for himself. Far less frequently are there dreams in which the dreamer is overtly aggressive; usually he is the target, but for 12-year-old Denise this is not the case:

> My most frightening dream ... Well, I woke up crying because I dreamt that I was a murderer and killed all my family.

She was shocked by the violence, the intensity of her antagonism. Animal-mad Claire (11) dreams, when she is ill, that she will die and 'never see my mum and dad and my pets ever, ever again'. She had another dream in which:

> I met some elves and they were bad but I never knew, they looked so innocent. I was losted and they offered me some bread and milk. It was poisoned. They started to run round in a circle saying, 'She's dead, she's dead, the little girl is dead.'

Louisa (12) has a nightmare in which her mother goes to work and never comes back. However, in another dream, her mother is having a baby. Is it possible that Louisa dreams about her mother having another baby as a way of keeping her at home? Quite a number of young people dream about having a baby brother or sister, and they are usually quite specific in the dream as to the sex of the sibling they want!

Some dreams are about a separation devoutly wished for, as is the case for Dawn (12). She lives with her mother and father and two brothers and described her happiest dream as one in which her brothers moved out and she 'had peace' and a room to herself!

Sleep-walking

Children report crying in their sleep but not often telling anyone about it. This is usually because they fear ridicule, or fear they will be dismissed as silly or babyish. Similarly, few talk aloud of sleep-walking, a sleep disorder rather than something which is directly dream-related. Yet children in my research reported sleep-walking even though I had not specifically asked about it. For instance, rugby-playing Phillip (13):

> I sleep-walk and my mum tells me that I leave all the lights on when I do.

These nocturnal walkers have no recollection in the morning that they have been sleep-walking and will usually vehemently deny it, as do those who talk in their sleep. It can be a very disturbing phenomenon; there have been a number of incidents reported in the Press in which adolescents, boys usually, have attacked other people or, as happened in one case, walked off a moving train while still asleep! If you have a sleep-walker on your hands, make sure your home is secure when you go to bed. Gently return him to bed when he wanders, and explore whether he is subject to any stresses that might be the cause of his rambles. Most young people grow out of it, but do ask for medical help if you feel the situation is beyond you. There may be a clinic in your area which specializes in sleep disorders.

Heaven, hell and the worlds between

Dreams in this category generally reflect the religious upbringing the child has experienced. Most examples in my research come from Northern Ireland children, as you will see, and show the intensity of their internalized beliefs. Possession by the devil causes most fear. Nora (14), from Londonderry, revealed her most terrifying dream:

> The devil was possessing my mother and then she was dying because of him. During the possession we stand by my mother and try to get rid of him. We don't succeed and I end up crying.

Eamonn (11) from Belfast:

> My mummy told me not to go near this house but I didn't do as I was told. When I went in the door jammed. A big demon appeared – he wanted my soul. Then I woke up shouting, 'You're not getting it!'

Instilled fear of the devil has been used as a means of making Eamonn conform. Some people say, 'The bogey man will get you,' bur Eamonn has learnt that the devil will get him if he does not do as he is told. Parents do use threats to make children conform, but beware, such fears can get out of control and severely disturb developing minds, for children may take you literally and believe that devils stalk them. That applies to Violet (11), a Catholic girl from Belfast, who dreamt that the devil appeared at the end of her bed and told her he would not go back to hell without her.

Claire (11), also from Belfast, has a recurring dream:

> I dream about fairies having a party. They fly up and down in the air. The queen of fairies is always sitting on her throne drinking wine and laughing all the time!

I noticed this quality of childlike innocence in many of the dreams from Northern Ireland, where there is much less superficial sophistication than can be seen in English city children. Children from Northern Ireland are more influenced by books and comics than their English counterparts. Claire flies in her dreams too, and like most children who have such dreams, loves the sensation of swimming, riding or gliding through the air. These dreams reveal a child's ability to escape the gravity, literal and metaphorical, of the world in which they live.

Cara (13):

My worst nightmare was when my friend Carole knocked at my door and I answered and she turned into a demon. My daddy came down and got the sledgehammer and knocked her over the head with it. Then she turned into a dog and I kept her.

In this dream Cara's father can control the evil that is present. He protects her and so she can keep this friend/animal that she had doubts about. Whether it is her friend she has misgivings about or a projection of her own 'demonic' qualities on to the friend, finally she will be alright because her father is in control; she can rely on him.

Dreams on this theme are not always unpleasant. Mildred (12), from Lancashire, dreams that she has a guardian angel who sits at the end of the bed to protect her through the night; while the happiest dream of Adrian (12) is of being in heaven with all his 'dead and alive relations'. He said, 'We are floating. We float on a bubble of sugar. In the bubble we see a light of blueish colour . . . I see my face in it. I look happy. Then I wake up.' These dreams give him a chance to re-experience pleasurable contact with relatives who have died and are a source of solace.

Coming to terms with heaven and earth can be a painful process as 13-year-old Daniel related: 'My most frightening dream was that I died and I found there was no heaven.'

Wish-fulfilment

Wish-fulfilment dreams continue throughout our lives, though the object of the desire may alter. Children dream of having animals of their own, being famous, never growing old and winning money. Nasreen (11), mentioned earlier, dreamt that she went to a children's theme park, went on all the rides and then 'saved the Queen from getting shot by an enemy'. For her efforts, the Queen invited her to live with her in a castle, to which Nasreen happily agreed! So, in this dream at least the role of rescuer has a reward.

Hayley (14) The starkly depicted dream of falling from a great height captures a common theme in dreams of children and adults alike.

Television soap operas have a high profile in dreams of this age group, particularly among girls. Sometimes the dreamer is in the soap opera with all the other characters, or having a close relationship with one of the characters. With boys, dream fantasies operate more around playing their favourite sport for a prestigious team and winning! Or, in Stephen's case, having a skateboard with all the fanciest embellishments possible!

Not all adolescent dreams are self-centred. Many reveal heroic tendencies, like 13-year-old Frank's: 'I dream about being rich and helping others who are poor – a bit like Robin Hood.' Eugene's (14) heroism fits the 'macho' pattern exemplified in many war films. He dreams of aerial combat with Messerschmitts in American deserts, and leading a Tomcat fleet; his happiest dream to date was when he killed all the 'enemy' single handed, with only 'a few air-to-air explode-on-contact missiles', Phew! Such dreams allow the safe expression of aggressive impulses, some of which are innate and some of which are fostered by violent images in comics and television.

This waking fascination with things military can be quite disturbing for Eugene. In his nightmares he dreams of being interrogated by the SS, being burnt alive and even being eaten alive. A dream he had about nuclear war was, he felt, too awful to dare describe.

Under attack

Joel (13):

> I have nightmares about being locked in a confined room with no windows, which I have once experienced, and I dream about my dog being put to sleep, which it was.

He also added, 'I'm not very intelligent. My life is in a mess. My brother beats me up. I don't do anything exciting and I never have any money or decent clothes.' He feels all this acutely, as the school he attends is very much a middle-class school, with affluent children and an emphasis on high academic performance.

Josiah (13) has also had a hard time and his emotional problems have meant a stay in a psychiatric unit. His nightmares about people changing into attacking demons indicate the parlous state of his self image:

> I was alone in the house and I heard a series of thumps on the stairs and I went and opened the door. In the doorway was my dad with cats all over his body and his nails were long and sharp and he slowly moved his hand towards me.

Fortunately Josiah woke up, thus saving himself from the ultimate terror. He also has recurring dreams of falling from the top of skyscrapers.

Elaine (12) described a dream in which her mother and father were king and queen of a hot country, while she and her sister were the two princesses, but all is not as it seems:

> In the country there is a conspiracy against the aristocracy and there is a weird killer out to kill us. He kills his victims by putting a long needle with dangerous poison in it in their heart.
>
> Then, one night I heard a noise in my sister's bedroom so I

ran in. A man was there with a long needle. I tried to stop him and jumped in front of Lisa and then he put a needle in my heart. Then I woke up and I felt a pain in my chest.

Elaine also has a lot of dreams in which her mother dies and she has to take over the family, which she does not like.

Elaine is the rescuer here but her role swiftly changes to that of the victim. Steve Karpman, an American transactional analyst, uses a triangle to describe life positions that people take up. While he relates this to adults, I feel it can be used to describe patterns of behaviour that children exhibit. The three points of the triangle represent the persecutor position, the rescuer position and the victim position. If we are flexible we can move from position to position; in Elaine's case she is moving but she is always on the receiving end of some kind of pain. Ultimately, helping children like Elaine to express and manage their fears means helping them to see that they are not just powerless victims.

Life changes

Lyn (14), a fairly typical 14-year-old, described herself as being pretty outgoing, but at other times she finds it really hard to get on with people. Sometimes, she says, she feels depressed:

That's when I have a bad dream. I quite often dream of death or of things happening to me or people close to me. Once I dreamt that I was knocked down and very badly hurt and everybody was crying and very sad. This dream took place when I was very unhappy as I'd just been arguing with my mum and my best friend.

It is significant that Lyn's parents separated last year and she is still affected by the accompanying major life changes; her father has gone, her living conditions have changed and her mother has been quite depressed. As we shall see in Chapter 8, Lyn's feelings are not unusual.

Dreams of death in adolescence in part reflect the increased suicide rates among adolescents, especially among those who have been experiencing stressful situations and where there is a history of serious mental health problems in the family. Doctors and psychiatrists in Britain deal each year with over 5,000 children under 16 who have tried to kill themselves. Dreams may be warning signals that parents and those who work with children need to heed, for while all who attempted suicide did not necessarily want to die, they did want to escape from the distress they were finding too hard to bear.

David (15) dreams about killing himself and described his earliest dream:

> The earliest dream I remember is jumping off a house and floating down. And then I tried it again and I still floated down so I kept on doing this until my dream ended.

John (14), who received expert care at the hands of Dr Michael Kerfoot, Principal Psychiatric Social Worker at Manchester's Booth Hall Children and Family Psychiatry Unit, had for some time dreamt about the class bully who viciously pursued him at school. Eventually he took an overdose of paracetamol but was found by his mother before lasting damage ensued.

If you are concerned about your child's mental health, listen to what he says about his dreams. If, allied to consistently distressing dreams, you see that your child is often tearful, depressed, seems unable to make close relationships, has problems with eating and sleeping, and there have been major life stresses such as moving house or illness and you have a gut feeling that something is deeply amiss, then get help. Go to a sympathetic GP who will spend time sensitively with you and your child. Find out if there are counselling services for young people in your area and get their support. As a family talk to each other and make time to get to know each other; as parents we need to invest a great deal of time in talking to our children. That is a very good, though under-used, preventive strategy.

Nightmares

The word nightmare originates in the medieval word for demon and all too often these 'demons' come to plague children at night, especially those around 13 and 14 years of age. These nightmares may frighten the still immature dreamer by their explicit violence or aggression, and many adolescents need education and reassurance about their dreams. For instance a 'wet' dream for a boy who has not been told about such events can be devastating. While few boys talk of night-time ejaculation related to dreams, this is to do with embarrassment about sex rather than an absence of such dreams. Explain to children that 'wet dreams' are not abnormal or injurious, but are merely part of the process of growing up. We will return to the subject of sexuality in dreams later in the chapter.

Nightmares often represent milestones in a person's development and can give us clues as to what new wishes, defences and skills are coming into play, though it may be that letting go of old modes of behaviour is hard to do, Mandy (14), from Stoke, dreamt that she was in a car with her mother when suddenly it crashed. Although Mandy jumped out and escaped, the car blew up and her mother was killed. Occasionally she has nightmares and returns to earlier comforting strategies:

I sometimes have nightmares but less than I used to. When I was younger and I woke up crying from them. I would go and get into my mum and dad's bed. When I have really bad nightmares now I still do this. If they are really bad, I can't get back to sleep, and shake with fear until I speak to someone, so I have to wake my mum or dad up.

For Neville (14), the worst nightmare he had ever had concerned sibling rivalry: 'I thought I had chopped up my sister and put her in next door's garden.' He was quite shocked to have had such a dream, yet they are not uncommon. Talking through feelings of anger and competition and giving reassurance to Neville would be beneficial.

Perhaps Sharron's 'most frightening' dream can give insight into the grim reality which influences some dreams in childhood. Aged 16, living in London, she has had a long experience of living in dire poverty;

When me mum had to go to hospital because she got a pram dropped on her head from the top of the flats, I dreamed that she died.

In her happiest dream:

My nan had come round to our house on Christmas morning and watched us open our presents like she always used to.

But her grandmother is now dead and her mother not yet recovered from living in poor housing, on little money and, as a marginalized member of our society, being rejected by many and supported by few.

Sue (15) has nightmares and needs some assurance, I think, to help her realize that she is not alone.

I'm really frightened to watch horror films or stay at home on my own. I even sleep with my bedside lamp on, I thought I would have grown out of it by now, but no, I haven't and I'm fifteen. I have nightmares about things I'm most afraid of, fire, thunder and lightning, animals and spiders and ghosts.

Wendy (14) from London dreamt that she went to her bathroom and:

I saw the ceiling round the light was red. Then suddenly blood started dripping from the ceiling and into the bath which was full of water.

There is a lot of symbolic imagery in this dream. The setting of the bathroom is important and makes me wonder if this dream relates to menstruation. Wendy's dream is visually very dramatic with dripping blood falling into the bath. Women do have different types of dreams according to where they are in their menstrual cycle, as my research for *Women Dreaming* revealed, and typically just prior to the onset of the period there are many more dreams of blood and savagery. It may be helpful to tell girls such as Wendy about this so they will feel less overwhelmed by their bloody dreams.

Jasper (15):

> I had a nightmare that all my family was being killed by a
> monster. The year was about 2500. It was sort of futuristic,
> like *Aliens*, I and my baby sister were the only ones to
> survive. I woke up in a sweat feeling sick.

He also said that dreams affect the way people continue their
daily life. If Jasper has a nightmare he usually feels on edge,
angry and moody. If the dream is pleasant he is unusually
cheerful; he knows dreams affect him a lot.

The distressing deaths of her two sisters combined with
family conflicts led Marcia (14) to a specialist unit for disturbed
adolescents. She had been stealing, fighting and generally causing
havoc at home and school. She now recognizes that her recurring
dreams about the traumatic deaths are because she blames
herself for them: 'I dreamt that my sister got killed, then I dreamt
that my little brother got killed in the same way.'

Anxiety dreams

Adrian (12), from Lymm, Cheshire:

> I often dream that I am in a crowded village, in the nude. I
> can see my friends and family. I see my enemies round me
> closing in and my family and friends are walking away. Just
> as the bad things close in the ground breaks and I fall down,
> down, down. I see a light getting bigger and bigger. Then I
> wake, usually about two in the morning.

I wonder if Adrian was born at 2 am? Midwives and others who
work with babies have told me that they notice children are
often fretful about the same hour that they were born, as if
recalling the birth trauma.

A common anxiety dream for Lisa (14) is that one by one her
teeth fall out. I came across this frequently in my research into
women's dreams where it usually reflected feelings of insecurity
about looks and separation, 'falling out' with friends and

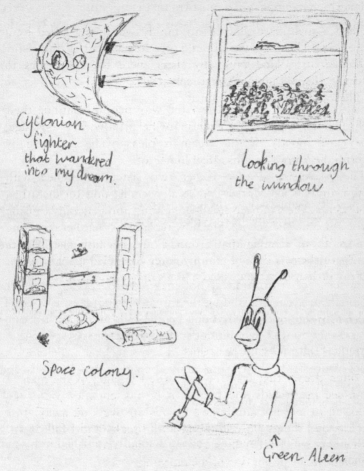

Cyclonian fighter that wandered into my dream.

looking through the window

Space colony.

Green Alien

Larry (13) *Space adventure and science fiction influence Larry's dreams.*

relatives. However it is not commonplace among the dreams of adolescents.

Rhiannon (14) was knocked down by a car and since then she has had dreams about being on a pelican crossing: 'I see the car coming towards me but it doesn't stop or hit me.' Her mother has told her that she bellows, 'Stop, stop!' from her sleep. This is another example of a post-traumatic nightmare. However, Rhiannon's other most impressive dream, a positive one this time, is:

> I'd be in a plane flying over seas and sometime during the flight the pilot would pass out and I would take over the plane and land everyone softly.

Incidently, she wants to join the RAF when she leaves school.

Chase dreams

Hannah (12), a happy successful extrovert, describes her dreams as usually connected to the daily events of her life. However, just now and then she has a typical 'chase' dream:

> Someone is running after me and no matter how fast I run the other person is always gaining on me but never catches me.

The sense of frustration at not making progress is there, but Hannah succeeds in avoiding the threat that pursues her. This is a healthy sign and when young people talk about such dreams you would do well to point out such positive aspects.

Other children who have such dreams feel more helpless, as does Anita (15). She dreams about being chased by bulls and always there is the ominous sound of the death-march being played. Cheung (15) dreams of:

> . . . being chased by men wearing black clothes and black hats . . . kept on following me and occasionally vanished into their hats.

In this dream, as in others, we would need to discover what Cheung associates with men in black hats who vanish into them! Our histories and cultural environment profoundly influence the content of our dreams.

Cheung also has recurring dreams:

> I have dreamt a couple of times about very narrow stairs which are extremely flimsy and often have steps missing, so I have to jump quite far to reach the next step.

These dreams of climbing staircases, going up in lifts and generally those involving going upwards, frequently relate to ambitions, be they work or academic. Such progress is not always easy and anxieties surface in dreams of this type.

Falling

We saw in Chapter 1 that as we drift into sleep, sensations of falling often occur and are a result of physical changes in the body; Siri (15), from the West Country, provides an example:

> Just as I'm dozing off, I picture myself in a bed falling down the stairs and then I wake up suddenly with a jerk, and find myself holding on to the side of the bed.

Many of Carrie's (13) dreams are externally triggered. For instance, she dreams of a bell and realizes that it is her alarm clock; she dreams of falling from a cliff and wakes up immediately to find herself grabbing her bed to prevent herself falling out.

> I dream I am walking downstairs and I miss a step and fall. I always wake up with a jolt, before I hit the floor. These dreams only last a few seconds, or at least I can't remember any more.

Carrie is afraid of falling downstairs and so her dreams reflect this.

Falling dreams are found at all ages and may signify feelings of being out of control or that we need to let go. The contents of the dream and the associations made by the dreamer will indicate if either of these fit. It is important to tell children that the superstitious notion that if you land in a falling dream you will die is untrue! Many young people, as well as a few adults, have asked me about this, believing if they hit the ground in the dream they would die.

Debris from the events of the day is identified as a major factor in dream content by 15- and 16-year-olds. Vanessa (15), for instance, said:

I had a cat who was 18 years old. She went missing last month. She is probably dead but because I don't know where she is I dream that she is alive.

When Vanessa is worried or upset, one of two dreams occurs:

Someone is in front of me telling me to come closer. The person has a smile on his/her face but the smile is false and sly. Everything is in darkness.

Or:

I'm being followed by a man and I come across a bridge and a deep canal. The man creeps up behind me and pushes me. I fall down into the river and I wake up as I hit the water.

When anxious she feels 'in the dark'. She feels unable to trust her senses and is propelled by forces outside her control. Her dreams express this symbolically.

Siri (15) dreams that he does not fall himself, but that his clothes do!

I dreamt I got up late and didn't have time to get dressed and so I went out with no clothes on and keep trying to get covers to cover me up, but they keep falling off.

Being stuck

Polly (14) talks of a 'gunman' in this dream, someone who only appears, in my research, in the dreams of Northern Irish children. Others talk of attackers or men with knives or maybe guns, but they are not described as gunmen. However, Polly's dream highlights the type of dream in which she is stuck, powerless to escape, or generally hindered from making any progress;

I was walking on a very lonely country road. It was dark at the time and suddenly I could see a gunman approaching me and I tried to run in the opposite direction. However, it was virtually impossible, as my legs just wouldn't move fast enough.

Ebony (16):

> I had a dream where gangsters were after me trying to kill me
> and I was running and getting nowhere. I tried to get to my
> house but they had killed all my family, including the dog.
> They had violin cases that dropped open like coffins for me to
> fall into!

In her nightmares, Ebony says she is always running and always
short of breath. This may be linked to her asthma, but we will
develop this aspect of dreaming in Chapter 5.

Being stuck, being suffocated and being paralysed usually
point to difficulties that the dreamer has with self-assertion.
Sometimes something as innocent-seeming as a bubble can cause
the problem, as it does for Angela (14):

> I dream of a bubble. It's not a soft bubble but it is hard and it
> has a heartbeat. It feels as if it is closing up on me.

Something with a living heartbeat is making her feel claus-
trophobic, causing her anxiety. Could it be easily dealt with,
easily 'popped', or does her passivity make action impossible?
Angela will probably be able to work on the dream and interpret
it herself.

Teresa described herself:

> I am a normal 15-year-old girl who cannot wait to be older to
> find a job and have a career. Nothing has really happened to
> me that was exciting. Yet sometimes I have felt that the whole
> world was against me and I have often broken down and
> started crying, yet I would never let anyone else see me crying.

This feels like a struggle that many adolescents go through and
yet it is so easy to overlook that pain which Teresa so eloquently
describes, and that sense of aloneness; that need to hide the
feelings away that make us so vulnerable. Adolescence is a stage
of change and vulnerability and dreams reveal this.

Dreams at this time often reflect the aggressive conflicts felt at
a deep level. Brett (16):

A lot are of fighting and running away from someone. Whenever these dreams occur, when fighting I can't punch properly, it's always in slow motion, it's the same with running.

Simon (16) described his most terrifying dream:

I was going upstairs and a woman with a knife was stabbing me and I was shouting my mum and dad but they did not come.

Simon is beginning to acknowledge that he is on his own, that he is becoming an adult and can no longer be dependent on his parents' interventions.

Robin (16) has a gratifying wish-fulfilment dream in which he plays his music to a large audience and they all appreciate it! Robin wants to be a professional musician and, after a recent split with his girlfriend, he spends most of his time playing. He said, 'I worry a lot about politics, murder and the future in general, but I usually put it to the back of my mind and get on with life. I have a very good relationship with my family and I talk to my parents about any problems. I think this is why I don't dream an awful lot about problems.'

Growing independence

The work of adolescence is to become independent, and adolescents have to grapple with coming of age in a complex world. They must find a way of separating from those who have thus far directed their lives. In doing so they become even more aware of the threats in the world. Gloria (13), from London, recognizes the fear of the streets shared by many women, young and old alike. She described one dream: '. . . I was walking alone in town and a man grabbed me and he raped and stabbed me. It was really horrible.' Though this dream terrified her she still felt that the worst dream she had ever had was one in which her mother left her.

Ina (13) also has street-fear dreams:

Me and my friend Emma was inside a chip shop . . . this

drunken man came in with a cigarette in his hand and he said he was going to burn us and the people who owned the shop was just laughing.

There is no support or protection for these girls.

Dreams during the 11- to 16-year-old period reveal the transition from dependence to independence. They show us the preparations that the young people undergo. Aggressive and impulsive themes increase, as do themes reflecting increased sexuality.

Sexuality

Major sexual developments happen during this time. Twenty-one per cent of girls will be menstruating by the end of their eleventh year, and by the end of the thirteenth year this figure rises to 80 per cent. At 15 almost all teenagers have reached physical sexual maturity and the vital phase of puberty is effectively complete at 16. Dreams are obviously affected by these changes, so for girls, for example, there is likely to be a significant increase in anxiety and hostility dream themes in the pre-menstrual phase.

Many adolescents feel that sex is a taboo subject as those who wrote to best-selling author Judy Blume explained in *Letters to Judy: What Kids Wish They Could Tell You*. They feel parents are embarrassed when it comes to sex, and leave their sons and daughters in confusing ignorance. However, the stages of sexual knowledge and development are seen in the dreams of those willing to volunteer them. You can see the development in the next four dreams.

Michael (11) dreams of ghosts, space and super-heroes, but he also has what he describes as 'rude' dreams:

The rude dream is about me getting a girlfriend and taking her to a disco and taking her to my place . . . .

No more details!

Claire-Louise (11) dreams of Michael Jackson coming to her

old school and singing. The high spot is when the idol: ' . . . is coming and kissing me and asking me to a meal. So I went and had a lovely time'. Russell (13): 'My happiest dream was when I dreamed I was abroad and me and the waitress found ourselves embraced.' Anika (14): 'Dreaming of dancing on an enormous stage, then making love with the man I'm dancing with. Usually someone I know.'

There were many dreams reported by girls which were suffused in a pink romantic glow; whether inspired by books, television or films, the rose-coloured fantasies continue! Renata (14) has a slightly different angle though:

> I dreamt about my honeymoon night. I was a man and I had to sleep in a pink bed with yellow wallpaper. But I didn't get round to doing 'it'!

Katy (12), from Rochdale, has vividly picturesque dreams of another land with waterfalls, long green grass and a golden palace in the heart of a verdant forest. In this setting her happiest dream occurs. A young servant marries the prince of the palace of gold, and they sit by the river every night in the full moon while an owl watches from a tree. The twist here is that Katy is the watching owl in the tree. She distances herself from the romantic events, and wisely, since owls symbolize wisdom, she watches and waits.

Marriage clearly has drawbacks in June's view. June (15) dreamt that she got married to a man in glasses and then: 'At the end of the wedding we climbed on to the top of the wedding cake and turned into plastic.' So, is she saying that you become 'plastic' upon marriage? That you lose feelings, become un-natural, rigid and transformed into unreal beings? Certainly June's dream indicates no warm, hazily romantic view of mar-riage so often portrayed in advertising and romantic fiction.

Adolescents of both sexes in Northern Ireland wrote of dreams in which they were happily married with a healthy family; these references to 'healthy, happy families' were quite pronounced. In mainland Britain, however, dreams concerned being married with a nice house and plenty of consumer durables. Moira (15) falls into the former group, coming as she does from Derry:

Me and my best friend met two boys and finally got married. We all lived together in my friend's house and we had children. But we all stayed the same age. Sometimes when we opened the door or looked out it would be a different place like a jungle.

It is as if they seal themselves off from the untamed, primitive world outside. They build their own cosy Utopia, free from ageing and free from interference.

Rape

Rhona (14) has many nightmares in which her vulnerability is highlighted. This one prompted changes in her waking behaviour:

I dreamt of being raped but an old boyfriend who was passing by stopped him (the rapist) and nearly killed him. The dream actually turned me against the guy that was raping me. I felt insecure whenever I would see him, and now, when I do see him, I make it short and sweet.

Subliminally Rhona must have registered fear about the man who rapes her in the dream. Although she did not recognize it while she was awake, her dreams have served to alert her to her unconscious knowledge. This does not mean that the man was actually going to commit the act, but that Rhona has some anxious feeling about him; part of her may see him as being overbearing and intrusive. This is what the dream dramatizes and as such it reveals the conflict that is causing disturbance to the dreamer.

Julanne (15), who is 'crazy' about the current number-one group, says she used to have a 'phobia' about her looks and going out, but is now getting over it. She never told anyone how worried she felt. Instead she kept all her feelings bottled up, as many adolescents do. As she lives far from her school, she does not have friends 'out of schooltime'. Fear is isolating. You can

Peggy (11) In her dream Peggy's guardian angel comes in the night to protect her.

tell from this dream how alone, and disabled, Julanne feels at times:

> ... the next minute I am in a wheelchair outside someone's house. The door opened and the handsome man was there. He said if he gave me an injection, I would be able to walk again. I am completely terrified about having injections and at school I go hysterical and start crying and screaming when I have any. The next minute I get up and go into the house ... I go down a long corridor with him and he leads me into a room and throws me on to a bed. He closes the curtains and then he rips all my clothes off me. He then rapes me through some kind of tube. All I can remember after that is that I am screaming at him to stop. I woke up crying and very shaken. I have never told anyone about this dream because everyone thinks that I am not the sort of person that would have these sort of dreams.

The fear that she might be seen as 'that sort of girl' isolates her, locks her into her fears so she does not have the chance to understand that many girls have anxious dreams about sex. She is not alone, nor need she be ashamed of such a dream. Dreams are neither 'good' nor 'bad', they do not have a rational code to guide them, but they can help us recognize fears that need airing. Julanne is unaided in the dream and being mechanically, almost impersonally raped; the tube is very phallic but also chilling. I wonder if this relates to any gynaecological examination she has had? They can certainly seem brutal, especially to one who is sexually inexperienced. I hope Julanne finds someone in whom she can confide; we all need at least one confidant.

In contrast, Estelle (15) is powerful in fighting off her would-be dream attacker:

> I had a nightmare in which a rapist broke into our house and I hacked him with a kitchen knife. I awoke abruptly at about 7 a.m. and went downstairs to lock all the doors. The dream really scared me.

This confident, outgoing young woman, is optimistic about the future and working hard at home and at school in order to achieve her ambitions. Her feelings of having control in her own life show in her dreams.

Monique (16) told me that her nightmares seemed always to be about men raping or attacking her. She said, 'I had one once where I woke up in a sweat because my dad, in my dream, had just raped me.' Holly (16) also dreams about being molested or raped, usually by people she knows. Other people are there but either do not hear her or else they do not help. The general insecurity in this dream was echoed in her other dream themes, such as either being in a big hole and being unable to get out or sitting on a very high wall, which is crumbling beneath her.

The dreamers may know whether fears are because of actual abuse; I say may because conscious knowledge of such traumatic experiences is often repressed in order to enable the child to survive. That which is hardest to accept we deny. Monique and Holly may have been abused. In Britain, according to the latest NSPCC figures 25,000 children every year are abused; 7,000 suffer sexual abuse. Other sources put the figure much higher, but whatever the figure, children are abused and most have nightmares about it.

There is another dimension we must not overlook. Sexuality is around in families and as children reach adolescence, as sexual maturity is reached, parents and offspring will be more aware of each other's sexuality. This is normal. As Skynner says in *Families and How To Survive Them*, 'There has to be the right amount of sexual feeling between the parents and the children . . . not too much and not too little.' Thus, the sexual dynamics within families may show up in dreams and it is helpful if young people can recognize those dynamics; it is part and parcel of growing up.

Ross (16), a sociable young man, concerned with issues in the world at large, is incensed by the 'gutter-level' attitudes to race and sex that he sees being pushed by much of the tabloid Press. He spoke of his dreams:

> Being of a volatile age, so to speak, it's obvious that some dreams will be sexually orientated. The dreams are never really X-rated, so to speak, and wouldn't entertain the boob-watching *Sun* readers of the world. If the dream is about sex then it isn't usually about a real person, more a sort of fantasy person and the dream reaches a 'climax'. I usually wake up before it gets good – the story of my life really!

Many adolescents dream of would-be sexual encounters which stop just before the longed-for climax, and Ross is certainly not on his own. Initial uncertainty of course occurs in the dreams of sexually inexperienced adolescents; however, factors other than sexual fulfilment are also involved. The need to impress, or at least be accepted by the peer group is important, for the peer group is a significant force in life at this time, as it is for Alex (16):

> I have dreams about a girl I liked very much and we met . . . I kept meeting people I knew and being proud because she was admired by everyone.

It is via the support of the peer group that most young people are able to break away from dependence on the family. Adolescents need to be able to choose friends and share confidences and experiences with them. They have to learn to negotiate, to make their own choices independently of parental pressures, and to make mistakes and learn from them. If they constantly rely on mother or father they will never be autonomous, and will forever remain dependent children. The role of the parent of course is to enable their children to become independent, and then let them go.

Michaela (15), like most young people, does talk about her dreams to her friends, especially if they feature in the dream dramas. Sometimes they have similar dreams and she says, 'That's OK because if you have what you might call "perverted" dreams, you feel pretty weird, like you hope you aren't the only one who has them. If you talk, you find other people have had them!'

Confidence building

Young people who took part in the research say that some dreams definitely boost their confidence, so much so that they have learnt to return to pleasant, fulfilling dreams each night, like watching a serial on the screen. Jennifer (15) explained how her dreams helped:

> In my dream I imagined that I was going to improve my looks. So in my dream I made my hair really lovely and that's what I did the next day after my dream … I have psoriasis and one night I dreamt of myself really working hard at putting my treatment on. So when I woke up I got the urge to always keep on putting on the cream, day and night.

Naomi (12) dreams of being a successful pop star and includes her friend as one of the supporting dream characters:

> I dream about being Denise from Five Star and winning loads of awards. And being really bonnie and glamorous. And even having my own dance studio like the Pineapple Studios.

In her pop-star dreams she sees herself in bright blue clothes while all the others are in dull greys, and the stage set is black and white. She really stands out, and the dream colour emphasizes this strong feeling of being special. In the dream she is successful, achieves her amibitions and wakes up feeling confident.

Dreams do help us to solve problems, as Isaac (15) discovered after playing a particularly difficult computer game:

> I didn't know how to get past a certain thing. I dreamt about doing it a certain way. I tried it and it worked.

Adolescent dreams in the Eighties

Faith (16), who takes on male roles in her dreams as do a number of female dreamers, gives a clear picture of adolescent dreams in the 1980s:

> I think my dreams depend on what is going on around me at the time. I quite often dream about karate because I go to a karate club. I have dreams about school and about my home and my family and my friends. When I dream most often my friends are the main characters and myself. This is probably because I have more fun with my friends.

Her most frightening dream pin-points a fear shared by many of her generation:

> It was about the world ending. The people on my street all came running out of their houses and yelling and I couldn't find my mum so I went to look for her. I went to Spar in the precinct and she was working on the till, even though she doesn't really. I wanted to save my mum. The next thing I can remember is counting down the seconds to the world blowing up.

This is an area we will return to in greater depth in Chapter 9.

It is not until adolescence that children are sufficiently independent to make an impact on society at large. However during adolescence we see major conflicts with the family almost as an unconscious testing ground for making changes in the wider world. The upsetting rebelliousness, difficult as it may be, is an important part of the development process, and necessary if the young person is to become an emotionally healthy adult. Not only that, as a society we need idealistic individuals to stop the rot that habit and complacency can bring about.

FIVE

Childhood Illness and Dreams

The early Egyptians and Greeks

The oldest dream book we have dates back to 2000 B C, and is from Egypt. The Egyptians practised dream incubation, that is sleeping in special temples in a deliberate attempt to induce inspirational, divine and healing dreams. Similarly in ancient Greece dreams played an important part in the process of diagnosis, prognosis and healing. Hippocrates – after whom the Hippocratic oath was named – Aristotle and Plato all believed that dreams revealed unseen workings of body and soul. Since that time there have been numerous studies showing that dreams do contain information about changes in the body and psyche before there are any overt symptoms.

It was not only diagnosis and prognosis of illness that concerned these early Greeks, but healing as well. There were 420 Asklepian temples at one time scattered throughout Greece, and when a person was ill she would go to such a temple, perform certain rites, sleep in a sanctified chamber and await a healing dream. It was believed that Asklepios, the god of healing, would appear in the dream and affect a cure. Nowadays such temples have fallen into ruins, but the power of dreams in relation to illness has not.

Why should dreams reveal the onset of illness, or indeed a cure? The answer is tied in with everything that has been said about dreams so far. Illness is an archetypal or universal condition and our unconscious responds to this as it does to any other life event. Changes in the body may be noted by the unconscious before our waking brains have noticed anything at all. Indeed such changes may be recognized in the dreams of family, friends or doctor before the 'patient' has an inkling of any change. Such dreams may be warnings of impending illness, or they may cause the dreamer to accept information registered on a subliminal level earlier in the day, or to face emotions repressed during waking hours.

Toni (12) described how, two days before she is sick, she dreams she is going to be ill, and how these dreams now act as a warning for her. Robert C. Smith, in his research with hospital patients, found that dreams do react to biologic functioning. Putting it very simply, he found that patients whose illnesses became fatal had significantly different dreams; men had more references to death while women had more separation references in their dreams. However, this does not mean that if you dream of death you have a fatal illness! Smith was actually studying the dreams of adults in hospital with life-threatening conditions.

Initial diagnosis

Meredith Sabini quotes research into illnesses as diverse as arthritis, cancer, migraine and multiple sclerosis, in which dreams have aided understanding of the development of the illness and the patient's attitude to it, including ways in which they have psychologically speaking been responsible for its onset and continuation. Work now undertaken at places like the Bristol Cancer Clinic, includes an examination of the way our life-style, mental outlook and capacity to relax affect health and illness. Dreams reflect these factors.

Migraine may start in childhood, and omissions of certain foods such as chocolate, cheese and citrus fruits can have a great effect in reducing attacks. However, dreams often warn of impending attacks. Pre-migraine dreams often involve aggression but also, in the majority of cases reported in one piece of research by H. Levitan, they involved situations of stark terror. If you regularly listen to your children's dreams you may find a pattern in which pre-migraine dreams feature. You can then see if you can circumvent the attack, or at least take steps to minimize its effect.

Treatment

Katy (12) has dreamt when ill that she is dying and that the only cure is a kiss from her mother! Remember the power of kisses to make hurts better? For Katy it appears there is still a great deal of investment in the power of her mother to heal her. Other children have other 'dream cures'.

Claire (11) has a lot of dreams about fairies who grant wishes. When she had influenza she dreamt that a fairy came through her window and threw magic dust over her. She said, 'When I woke up in the morning I was completely cured. Bethany (7) dreamt of going to heaven and speaking to her grandad; that made her feel better straight away. Support from those whom they love is very important to children, especially sick children. And it does not matter if the person the child dreams of is dead. What is important is to recognize that the love of that person has been internalized by the child, and she carries it around inside like a talisman to combat misfortune.

Nathan (11) is certain that his dreams are therapeutic:

> I dream of getting better and the dream normally has some-thing to do with it. For example, when I broke my arm I imagined being a weight-lifter.

This dream seemed to strengthen his arm and he was optimistic about his dream-assured recovery. This would be a very useful technique to encourage other children to use. It is empowering and goes along with the holistic approach to health which recognizes that mind and body work together to combat illness.

Germaine (9) always has warrior dreams which leave her feeling more confident that she will fight off her attacking illness. Modern research into pharmaceutical products and their effects has not been altogether reassuring. Many drugs have directly caused death or handicap (opren and thalidomide, for example) while others (like the contraceptive Pill and children's aspirin) have given widespread cause for concern. Such informa-tion may become known to children, or a natural resistance to outside chemical interference filters through; but whatever the source of awareness many children's dreams reveal a distrust of doctors and their remedies. For example, Karen (12) dreams that the medicine prescribed is poison and will kill her.

Fear of dying

Derry (11) made a heartfelt plea for understanding and support when he knew I was writing this book. He asked me to tell parents that, 'When a child is ill he has very bad nightmares.' Derry only has nightmares when he is ill and then he usually dreams that he dies. Dreaming of death during illness is not at all uncommon for children. I found 40 per cent of 13-year-olds, for instance, had dreams of dying when they were ill. Yet such fears are so easily overlooked. As Simon Yudkin, Consultant Paediatrician, said in his *Lancet* article 'Children and Death', 'Some children who are ill are afraid of dying. They should be given the opportunity to show their fears and to talk about what death means to them so that the origin of their worries can be made clear and so they can be reassured.'

The range of 'death' dreams during illness is often morbid; Xanthe (13), when she is ill, dreams that she will die of a deadly disease, or that someone in her family will die; Samantha (11) has especially sad dreams in which she dies 'without saying Goodbye'. Gareth (12) dreams of his coffin and funeral, while Tracey (11) dreams 'that I stop brevin' and I die'. Tabitha (12) dreams that she wills all her money to her parents. She explained that when she is ill she always thinks about dying, so, 'because I have it on my mind during the day, I dream about it at night'.

These dreams of death during illness would seem to have a very negative effect, but for Sally (13) this is not the case, for her dream of dying when ill '. . . is a funny sort of dream, yet I never die in it. I wake up upset and it gives me a will to get better'.

Kelly (11):

When I was ill with my throat I dreamt that I was going to swallow my tonsils and choke on them. Then I dreamt I was going to die because I had nothing to drink and I was choking. My face went blue and I died.

Perhaps just a simple explanation of how infections cause swellings would help Kelly. She would understand that although she feels as if she is choking, she can still breathe because other airways are open for her and that her tonsils cannot become detached as they do in the dream. Such knowledge alleviates much of the mental stress present at the time of illness simply because children are naturally ignorant about how their bodies work.

The content of dreams highlights the nature of the illness in many cases. When she is ill, Linden (11) dreams that she is going to drown. When she is sick her throat is always sore. She thinks she is drowning because she cannot breathe easily and feels as if she is choking, spluttering and fighting for air, as she would be if sinking under water.

Images in illness

Abstract forms of colour and shape are very common in the dreams of sick children. Tiffany (12), from Cheshire, dreams of lots of colours spinning round until, all of a sudden, she drops and wakes up. Louise (11) dreams of 'colours whizzing round like a whirlwind', but additionally, 'writing appears on the bedroom wallpaper'. Andrew (11) combines these elements in his dreams during illness: 'I dream of patterns like white paper with red, purple, green and other colour blotches.'

Things become less clear, unfocused, indicating perhaps changes in our ability clearly to differentiate objects and ideas when we are ill. Certainly there is less energy and inclination to do so.

Sometimes the colours are linked to a threat of some kind, as Alison (12) knows:

> My Mr Men curtain design changing into coloured blobs, coming out at me. In the background there was a man laughing and always there was a creamy white sheet of BIG paper that got blackened and dirtied which distressed me.

This was the earliest dream she could remember and it still recurs when she is ill.

Ingrid (11) had a recurring dream during illness which started when she was much younger. It too involves swirling round very fast, only it is in darkness, but 'all of a sudden it would go so bright that I couldn't see. I would be going towards a brightly coloured triangle and just as I'm about to hit it, I wake up'.

Unusual qualities of light feature in many dreams during illness. Neville (14), for instance, has a frightening dream when he is ill, in which a thin line of light shines in his unlit room. There is someone on the line of light and it is as if a string of rocks is trying to snap it. When he wakes up the dream is still there and he continues to see the line of light. Physiological changes in the body probably cause this type of dream, particularly if a high temperature is present.

Kevin (11) has a recurring dream that small rocks, then larger rocks, come rolling down a hill to the bottom, where he is tied up. Before they hit him he wakes up. The dream reveals his sense of powerlessness. He cannot prevent the onslaught, just as when 'run down' we have not the strength to combat infection. Another kind of invasiveness is depicted graphically in David's (9) dream where he is 'in a land with green dust everywhere and green swampy slime dripping down from the trees'.

Feeling alone

Robert (13) has very few pleasant dreams; most reveal some kind of threat and isolation, but this is especially the case when he is ill:

> When I am ill I dream that I have got the black plague and nobody will go near me.

Rather than being comforted and treated with extra tender loving care, Robert feels rejected. Other children have dreams in which there is no source of support or care: Edgar (16) dreams that he is trapped in space and is being chased, crushed and spiked by unknown, unrecognizable objects. In a less dramatic dream Melody (10) is boxed in and short of air, and she feels scared about what is happening outside; nowhere feels safe.

Illness does separate us from others, not just in the event of quarantine, but just because we cannot do the ordinary things we normally do. Illness debilitates us. Children find this quite overpowering at times, partly because, with young children in particular, their sense of time is not developed and the duration of the illness seems like eternity. Saying, 'You'll be better in a couple of weeks', usually works to soothe and reassure adults, but with children, daily reassurance and progress reports are called for. I think Shaista (11) catches the mood of being 'kidnapped' by illness very well.

> When I am ill I dream about scary things like catching a very bad disease. Once I dreamed that I had to swap teeth with a man who kidnapped me. The teeth kept falling out so I had to use Superglue to stick them in.

She is being forced to give up her own 'teeth', symbolically used to denote strength, and use another person's teeth. Is this 'other' the doctor? Whatever or whoever it is, she needs additional help in order to retain her 'bite'. However, the dream has an optimistic atmosphere as she assertively finds a solution; she literally sticks with it!

Childhood ailments

When children have high temperatures and feverish symptoms, intensely vivid dreams are often recalled. Many children spoke of the different quality of such dreams. Roxanne (16), for example, said:

> When I am very hot or feverish I always have the same dream in which everything is very distorted and somehow larger that it should be. When I was young I used to dream about a mute swan, and I remember feeling scared because like the swan, I couldn't call out.

Virginia (11) told me: 'I dream that my body is being burned and I am still alive and trying to get out. Then I wake up.' And

Duncan (9) related that: 'Sometimes when I'm ill I dream about a huge bonfire and a clock. I fly into the clock and I can't breathe.' So the symptoms felt physically are translated into fiery images which simultaneously depict the anxiety to which the child has fallen prey.

Norfolk-born Alice (12) dreams, when ill, that there is something in her mouth and often her hands and face feel like marble. She dreams that everything must be straight or flat, just perfect in fact. She also has many dreams about fire when she has a high temperature, but with Alice, another fear is incorporated, as she explains:

> This is true and I have to tell you it to understand my dream. One harvest a field in our village was being burnt, the straw, and it got out of control. Everyone in the village went to see what was happening. I was very small then and my dad went up on to the verge and lifted me up to watch the fire. I was absolutely terrified. Then the fire suddenly came very fast towards the verge and in a minute the verge was on fire. Dad jumped back in time but I was very scared.

Alice went on to describe one of the variations of her fire-dream theme:

> I was playing in the field and somehow it was on fire in a second. When I tried to get away it took me a long time to get to the road. When I got on the road it was spreading very quickly towards the road. It ended then though.

Her fire dreams come when she is hot, unwell and feeling vulnerable.

Chicken-pox
Chicken-pox is a nasty childhood disease and one which all of my three children have suffered from. My 5-year-old daughter was very frightened when she saw the 'pox' popping up and thought they would never go away! It took much reassurance to persuade her that she would not be covered in the painful

blisters for ever. Charlotte (7) had her most frightening dream when she came down with chicken-pox, and it seems to sum up the physical aspect of the illness. She said she was being chased by a giant:

> In my dream, every time I hit an island, it went bump! And then I hit another island and it went bump!

This went on all night and when she woke she was covered in her 'bumps'.

When Rosemary (13) was 8 she too had this illness, and a terrifying dream:

> The dream started in my sleep but I woke up and it carried on like an hallucination. It was like trees and enormous plants grasping at me, trying to hold me, trying to kill me. I screamed but it didn't go and I was wide awake. It carried on until my mum came in and turned the light on. I was really upset and scared.

The edges between dreaming and waking reality here are blurred as can happen when a person has a very high temperature.

There is another physically manifested event known as the Isakower phenomenon, which occurs most often in childhood and adolescence. Though it usually happens as the young person is falling asleep, it can happen at other times. There is a dry sensation in the mouth and on the hands and skin, and a shadowy visual aspect is present; the sleeper feels a blurring of their own body and the world. This is quite a rare phenomenon, though some individuals can produce it at will. Should your child experience it during illness or at any other time, reassure her that she is not going crazy, that other people have had it, and that it is temporary and will pass.

Going to hospital

Going into hospital can be very upsetting for children and may cause severe anxiety. Children who are separated from people

Rosie (9) The drawing shows Rosie sleep-walking. Once she 'walked' outside her house so now, her mother keeps the front door key under her pillow.

they trust and love and thrust into an alien environment are frightened. Frequently they fear that they will be physically hurt or changed and such an experience can be very damaging if not handled sensitively. This is not a new finding. In 1945 Levy was the first child psychiatrist to recognize the significance of recurrent nightmares following operations. He compared the effects of the battlefield with the 'surgical field', both of which may cause severe trauma expressed in nightmares.

Psychologist Lindy Burton describes the recurring nightmare

of a 19-year-old student, which she traced to an experience at 3 years of age. The girl believed that the emergency operation for appendicitis had maimed her:

Like so many other small children subjected to unexplained and often frightening illness and treatment procedures, she had evolved a fantasy in which her surgery had subtly but permanently damaged her.

Some children fear that the anaesthetic will kill them or that the nurses want to harm them, administering, as they have to, unpleasant treatments. Later, lingering fears may be expressed directly in words, or more obliquely in behaviour. We can see this when children are so agitated that they cannot be still, when they have angry outbursts or look scared or withdraw into isolated shells, cutting themselves off from others. Similarly, a child who suddenly starts wetting or soiling the bed when she is normally dry, is communicating her distress by the change in behaviour.

These fight (angry outbursts) or flight (withdrawal) behaviours are classic mechanisms for drawing attention to fears, and can alert adults to distress. A child may feel a great sense of helplessness in illness, as if she has no control over her body or her life. It is a very frightening sensation and, if left unaided, it can lead to hopelessness which further works against regaining health. Studies of the immune system show that the psychological willingness to combat disease brings about a high degree of successful rejection of illness, while passive acceptance is much less favourable in terms of recovery. Helping our children to rebuff illness mentally is a health-giving strategy which should last them all their lives.

Many young children who have to receive hospital treatment feel anger with parents, especially the mother, because they expect her to be all-powerful and able to protect them from people they believe hurt them. The mother may be seen to fail because she did not stop the pain or operation, and left the child with strangers. John Bowlby, eminent child psychiatrist and psychologist, rescued many children from the lonesome fate of being abandoned in hospital. His research and writings led to the change in climate that enabled parents to have unrestricted visiting with children, and indeed won the right for parents to sleep in hospitals while their child receives treatment. We will return to Bowlby's work in Chapter 8.

In *Emotional Care of Hospitalized Children* M. Petrillo and S. Sanger discuss the case of 5-year-old Ruth. Ruth developed nightmares after cardiac surgery in America. When returned from intensive care forty-eight hours after her operation, she refused to sleep because she was having terrifying nightmares. Obviously Ruth was reacting to the ordeal of the operation and trying to work through her experiences in her sleep.

Medication and reassurances that she would be alright failed to ease Ruth's sleep problems, so her mother and nursing staff worked together to solve the problem through play activities. She was encouraged to face the dream fears by imagining that there was another little girl coming into hospital and by preparing some pictures and a small booklet for her to explain what would happen. She also played with special dolls, giving countless play injections, inserting and removing chest tubes and so on. Sometimes she played the doctor, sometimes the nurse, or even the patient. Within two days, the nightmares disappeared. The rest of her convalescence went smoothly and her mother continued the play therapy after discharge so that Ruth could continue to act out any remaining fears that might be lurking undisclosed.

After hospitalization many children experience sleep disorders. Yet it is not a subject that hospital staff tend to talk about, so parents are unprepared for the difficulties that arise. In a way they are part of the recuperation process; listen to the dreams, let the child talk out her fears or draw or play them. As Ruth's mother found, actively facing the fears dispels them, if it is done with love, sensitivity and patience.

Asthma

Childhood asthma attacks often occur during the night, and studies have shown that upsetting dreams play a part in their onset. If the child has had a stressful, conflict-ridden day, then she is likely to have this material in her dreams. In turn the dream may provoke an asthmatic attack. Clearly, physical factors are important triggers too, but psychological factors are known to be critical in the illness. Particularly relevant is the relationship with parents. Twice as many boys suffer from asthma as girls, and this seems linked to their feelings of aggression and deep conflicts, which we looked at in earlier chapters, for the active expression of aggression in dreams seems to contribute to the production of asthma attacks.

If you can bring these feelings into the light of day and deal with them openly, difficult as this may be, you may help your child avoid night-time asthma attacks.

Dream imagery in visually impaired and disabled children

As a child Marjorie had a tendency towards nightmares and night terrors. Now a doctor, she understands why this was so:

> They may have arisen from severe short-sightedness; as neither parent has this, they did not know that when I took my glasses off to go to bed, everything swelled and blurred and harmless objects could acquire a terrifying aspect.

These comments are worth bearing in mind if you have a short-sighted child.

Blind and disabled children dream about many of the same things that sighted children do. They dream of television characters and cartoons, of animals and family, of flying and wish-fulfilment delights and they also have nightmares. They have dreams of illness as do their peers; however, their handicap has a definite influence on the nature of their dreams.

Children who lose their sight between their fifth and seventh years may still have visual images and REM periods during sleep, but if sight is lost before the fifth year there is no dream vision, as J. Jastrow noted as long ago as 1888. The congenitally blind cannot visualize; they have no rapid eye movement during otherwise normal REM periods. Usually they describe their dreams in tactile or auditory terms. My interviews with many young people at their school for visually impaired children confirmed this.

Shamina (14) reads braille and can see shadows and outlines but nothing distinctly. She had one dream of an amorphous ghost eating her up which is characteristic of the vague, ill-defined shapes found in the dreams of most visually impaired people:

> When I was ill and my mother was sleeping in the other bed, the ghost was all white, wouldn't go. Lots of sheets on him. I thought he had lights.

Shahzad (13) can see only in daylight. He told me:

Last night I dreamt of a haunted house, saw vampires and ghosts. I panicked and fainted, then someone picked me up. I woke up and saw lots of vampires trying to turn me into a frog ... I found magic books, I said Abracadabra and Hocus Pocus, and changed the vampires. There were skeletons, I could hear their bones and chains rattling and the sound woke me up.

Shahzad's basic self-confidence comes through in the dream where in response to each threat he finds a means of escape.

Janet (11) has damage to the back of her eye. She can see long distances but has problems with close vision. Her wish-fulfilment dream reflects her desire for her chronically ill sister to be made well:

> I went to see the Queen with Prince Edward. I was scared. She was a bit annoyed because one lot of visitors had just left and she wanted to relax. I wanted her to help my sister by sending a rich doctor, because my sister has to have very expensive medicine night and day.

Notice how she is sensitive to being a nuisance to the 'Queen' figure. This could well represent female authority figures to whom she feels she is a burden. However, her need to get help overrules such concerns and she has a helper in the male prince figure.

Males are prominent characters in Janet's dreams. She told me that she has 'rude' dreams about boys she meets at the youth club:

> When I have sex with a boy in bed in a dream it is happy. I enjoy it. After a bit I have a baby, he leaves me to go to work and he goes to the pub. I want a night out with the girls but he won't stay in.

She shrugged her shoulders and added, 'Boys are like that.'

Janet feels afraid and alone in many of her dreams and would like someone to confide in; she never talks to anyone about them though, especially not her mother because, 'She'd say they are disgusting.' Shahzad tells his mother about his pleasant dreams. Usually she says, 'very nice', but he protects her from others because 'she doesn't like frightening things'. Another little girl at the school never talks to anyone about her dreams because, 'they're special and they belong to me'.

It is important to bear these comments in mind when talking to children about dreams since they may have received all kinds of prescriptive messages which make it difficult to speak of their dream life. Respect of privacy is also very important and no child should ever be forced to reveal dreams they wish to keep secret.

Gervaise (11) had an unusual dream:

> I dreamt I got run over and the next day I did get run over. It was on a pelican crossing exactly the same as in the dream. I thought it was the dream again. I used to dream about hospital a lot after that.

He may have dreamt this because of an unconscious fear of this crossing, or because of auditory clues that were causing alarm; it may have been because of some kind of premonition, but we will return to that idea in Chapter 6. However, Gervaise, like so many children, does not speak to anyone of his very upsetting school-related dreams in which he is running away from school because people are picking on him.

Susan (8) has severe tunnel vision and can only see out of the corners of her eyes. She describes a disturbing dream:

I dreamt about pulling my eye out. Mum put it in the bin and rubbish got on it. And then I went blind. She took it out and gave it to me, then I stuck it back in . . . Funny dream.

Children do dream specifically of their visual handicap, though I found it unusual. Research reviewed by blind psychologist Donald Kirtley revealed that with adults, when blindness is the result of traumatic injury, there is much post-trauma dreaming as the dreamer comes to terms with what has happened. In some cases the action of the dreams proceeds up to the point just prior to the injury taking place, as if in her mind the dreamer stops the worst happening. Such dreams may continue for many years.

Javed (8) has heroic dreams of fighting for Robin and Batman against the Penguin, helping friends or foiling robbers. But he found one of his dreams particularly sad:

Mum was going away because she didn't want to live at home anymore. I followed them. Everyone [in the family] was going. Then they went to the motorway, then I got lost. They left me behind. There was no one to look after me.

Javed, like many blind people (especially children, of course) is very dependent on those around him, particularly his family, and at times this arouses fears about what would happen if they should disappear. Here Javed's dream expresses his concerns. If dreams were 'on the agenda' and openly discussed in the small tutorial groups at Javed's school for instance, there would be the opportunity to acknowledge and work through such widely felt fears.

Profound limits in freedom of mobility influence the dream settings of visually impaired people. Familiar places, such as home or the immediate environment, usually figure prominently, reflecting the fact that going to strange locations is much more problematic than it is for the fully sighted. Javed's dream quoted above is unusual in that he does go far afield, but we must take into account his grave anxiety about being deserted; the ultimate fear forces him to take more risks.

Sounds are all important in the dreams of blind and partially sighted children, Jamie (3), an albino child, who can hardly see at all, generally likes dreaming and currently dreams of his dog fighting off a bad dragon. When I asked him how he knew his dog was there he told me he heard the loud growls. Similarly, Leon (9), whose mother contracted rubella while pregnant with him, relies on the senses of touch, smell, taste and movement to inform his dream world. Using an amplified hearing aid and carrying a microphone into which those who speak to him communicate, he can take part in lively conversations. Though blind from birth his dreams are vivid with sensation, texture and sound. His favourite dreams are of going to the local West Indian gospel church with his auntie, because those dreams are filled with music, singing and clapping. Less warmly received is a dream of a witch who puts him on her back and flies on her broomstick. Sometimes the witch tries to eat him; he can feel and hear her.

Leon also has nightmares, he said:

> I feel frightened. Cry sometimes. Bad bears are swearing at me and being horrid. Sometimes I am being attacked and someone is trying to kill me. Once they hit me so hard I could feel the sword that was being used.

When he was ill with German measles, he dreamt of a dog trying to bite him and, as many children caught in the isolating fear of nightmares, he sought refuge and company in his mother's bed. He only ever does this if his father is on night-shift because, he remarked gloomily, his father has no sympathy and packs him straight back to his lonely room.

We will see in a later chapter the great influence television has on the dreams of children, and while blind and partially sighted children are no exception, in their dreams the visual imagery is replaced by tactile and auditory sensations. Linda (10) dreamt of being stabbed by Freddy from *A Nightmare on Elm Street*; Hiram (8), who has had a number of operations for cataracts since he was a baby, feels the Snow Queen putting pieces of ice in his heart. The film really frightened him when he was taken to it last year. However, like many boys he has happier hero-worship dreams where he aids a famous TV 'goodie'.

Oscar (11) also suffers from cataracts, and was scared after *Jaws*. He said:

> I saw it in my head, the boat being smashed. I got killed. I get pictures in my head and eventually my brain doesn't want the picture so it eats it up. In my dreams my sight gets blurred and then I wake up.

He also said that his story-tapes influence his dreams, especially stories like *The Secret Seven*. His friend Mark (13), who can read large print and distinguish colours in spite of very poor sight, dreams of TV cartoon characters. In one dream he fights a monster: 'It was awful. It felt like, soft and yukky! . . . Usually when I have a bad dream I go into the bathroom and wash my face. That helps.'

Other disabilities

As with visual impairment the range of dreams of deaf children depends on the extent of their disability. Daily events and personal relationships influence the content of their dreams as much as they do the dreams of children who are not disabled. Again, the critical period for auditory memory extends from the age of 3 to 7. Deafness prior to age 3 usually results in muteness too, a factor that will be reflected in the child's dream life. Motor-activity is of major importance in the dream content.

Helen Keller at 19 months contracted scarlet fever, which left her totally without sight, hearing, smell and speech. Aged 6 she began learning to communicate using the then popular finger alphabet. In 1904 she became the first deaf-blind person to receive a degree. In her autobiography, *The World I Live In*, Helen Keller devoted two chapters to her dream life. She said she had sensations, aromas, tastes and ideas that she did not remember having experienced in waking reality. These may be remnants from infancy or intuitive knowledge. She found that her dreams were compensatory, for she had increased physical freedom and was more independent in her dreams than in her waking life.

Whenever there has been 'normality' followed by sudden disability physical or mental, dreams will attempt to come to terms with the drastic changes imposed. Most research to date has been done with adults, but we have no reason to believe that the findings would not apply to children. For instance, J. Jastrow found that individuals who had become crippled or undergone amputation of limbs in late childhood or as adults, continued to dream of themselves as physically whole for some time after the amputation. The 'phantom limb' remains in dreams.

Mental retardation

As noted in the first chapter REM sleep is important for cognitive processes. In mental retardation there are difficulties with the mechanisms that enable learning to take place, and, according to I. Feinberg, in most instances REM sleep is severely curtailed when compared to non-handicapped children.

Ten-year-old George, who has Down's Syndrome, was the only boy in the study who admitted having wet dreams. These were about his girlfriend at school. Whether his candour was because he did not feel at all embarrassed about them I do not know. I do know that he found them enjoyable and much nicer than his frightening dreams about snakes! Perhaps the snakes were a more threatening aspect of his sexuality.

Again the ubiquitous ghosts and TV characters appeared in George's dreams as they did in other children's at the special school he attended.

Psychological and emotional ill health

Of course, not all illness is physical. Some young people suffering great emotional strain shared their dreams with me and recurring themes were death and emotional pain. Harry told me how life was for him:

My name is Harry Smith. When I was 13 I got put into care because my dad was on drugs and my mum was an alcoholic but then my mum got a job but I was in children's homes and with foster parents for a year. Last week I went back home and since I have been home I have been glue-sniffing and I have to talk to someone.

On a good night he dreams that all will be well and he will be better soon. But more frequently his dreams are about being shot, his family being hurt and also being unable to move when he is being chased. Harry is stuck and feels powerless both in his dreams and in his family. His most frightening dream depicts with disturbing intensity a journey to the depths:

I dreamt I was going down in the lift of the block of flats where I used to live. The lift would go down past the ground floor. Blood dripped out of the ventilator. The lift stopped and the door opened. Something was there but I couldn't see. I screamed but no sound came out.

At the time of writing, Harry is back in the adolescent hospital unit, which will try to enable him to experience more positive ways of being in the world. This can be a monumental task when the emotional damage inflicted has been so destructive for such a long time; it is like learning to live all over again. Dreams are used in supportive psychotherapy with adolescents and are especially helpful in the treatment of intense, often unconscious, emotional conflict, typical of this age group. Using dreams as part of the therapy process, young people can learn about the complexities of relationships, particularly family relationships, and find ways of cutting the ties that bind in a less destructive manner. Understanding leads to decreased feelings of being out of control and increased self-awareness and self-confidence. Dreams can also be used as markers to the changes that are taking place in the adolescent and, if kept in a sequential way, provide a picture of important themes and ways in which they have altered over a treatment period. Additionally they can illuminate and strengthen daily life by putting the dreamer in touch with revealed positive attributes.

How do therapists work with dreams? Although there are

Marie (8) In her dreams Marie relives the traumatic time when her brother suffered a severe head wound.

many different styles, or theoretical orientations, at the simplest level many use the methods described at the end of Chapter 3. Children and adolescents can be asked about the associations they make with their dreams, the emotion they display in them, the feelings they have about other characters who feature, and any other material in the dream. Much can then be inferred by child and therapist about the message of the dream. However, it must always be borne in mind that interpretations should not be forced on the dreamer; instead he should be enabled to consider the dream, as far as he wishes to go with it, in a safe, supportive, non-judgemental atmosphere.

The REM state is influenced by personality disturbance, for instance in depression, alcoholism and psychosis. E. Hartmann and his co-workers concluded, after considering research in this area, that higher REM states happen in association with states of 'psychic pain', or at times of psychic imbalance when the dreamer attempts to change customary defence patterns. Thus quite often the person who requires more R E M sleep is relatively anxious or depressed and there are changes in her life-style about which she worries. Nina (14), who lives in a professional middle-class family, is very happy most of the time. But now and again she has mood swings and the following nightmare came when she was quite depressed and sleeping for long periods:

> I dreamt that my mum and dad turned against me and wouldn't let me into the house. All my friends had turned against me. I was all alone. I started crying and then I killed myself.

E. Rossi argues that this need for increased R E M sleep is because of chemico-biological changes which are occurring in the brain as proteins are synthesized. This area of psychosynthesis research may open new doors in the understanding of how mental health can be further developed in dreaming.

Sleep disturbances such as nightmares and sleep-walking are frequently a response to a traumatic event in the child's life. If these symptoms of distress are ignored for an extended period the child may become further incapacitated by neurosis. Parents can help by discussing things with the child and encouraging her to express her feelings in an open way rather than repressing them. In cases where expert help has been sought for sleep problems such as these, many different techniques may be used.

Leonard Handler, an American therapist, described the way he worked with an 11-year-old boy diagnosed as emotionally disturbed and minimally brain-damaged. For about a year and a half John had been having terrifying nightmares; he would wake up in a panic and rush to his parents' room to seek comfort. The monster in his dreams chased him and sometimes caught and hurt him.

In order to ameliorate the situation, Handler, who had developed a good rapport with the boy, used confrontation therapy. Using this method the child was asked to sit on the therapist's knee, thus providing physical proximity and security, and then, having been reassured that they would fight the monster together, the boy was asked to close his eyes and visualize it. When he said he could see it, the therapist held him more closely while pounding on the desk and shouting something to the effect, 'Get away from my friend you lousy monster! If you come back I'll be with John and we'll fight you.' This was repeated a number of times, with John eventually feeling empowered to join in the 'seeing-off' of the monster.

When asked in the next session whether he had seen the monster, John replied that he had but had yelled at it and the fearsome beast had disappeared! Six months later the nightmares had still not returned. This fantasy technique can be used by adults who have a strong trusting relationship with a child.

Abuse

Abuse of children happens in all social groups; it is not restricted to the poor and ill-educated. And those who are abused often deal with the trauma in dreams. To date, most research has been with the one-to-one psychoanalytic field. However, much work needs to be carried out into the way in which dreams inform 'carers' that a child is being abused.

According to H. Maisch, incest victims suffer nightmares or other sleep disorders. Jean Goodwin of the University of New Mexico Department of Psychiatry described how drawings of dreams are used both to ascertain the nature of the abuse and to enable the child to work through the damaging experiences she has been subject to. One 9-year-old girl drew a dream picture of herself in a wedding dress standing in front of a house in a field full of flowers. She talked to the therapist about her dream, and spoke of her longing for a new father and a new marriage for her mother, and of her fear that her mother would not be able to divorce the father who had committed incest. Goodwin commented on the fact that flowers may be used symbolically by girls who feel 'de-flowered', as in this dream. She had worked with one very depressed and abused 7-year-old, who drew page after page of drooping flowers which had been stripped of their petals.

Many abused children feel utterly distraught and confused when they are subject to sexual abuse. The confusion arises in part because they see an adult as an authority figure and yet they have been forced to do something wrong by that authority. So somehow, the action must be alright. At a gut level victims feel it is wrong, but they cannot argue against the emotional and physical pressure that is applied. Many nightmares will reflect severe anxiety about being chased, perhaps by big, heavy creatures such as elephants, and being unable to escape, unable to do what they want to do; thus the element of force is prevalent.

Jan, now in her forties, told me of a recurring dream she had from the age of 9 to 12:

> I was in a vast dark hall. The floor was white and black squares like a chessboard and there were four staircases, one in each corner, going nowhere. Light came from above like a dull spot-light. At the top of each stairway stood a man in robes – no faces visible. I was thrown from one figure to the other, not necessarily aggressively but each time I was not confident I would be caught. Each figure held me briefly and passed me on. No sound.

The dream began after she was first subjected to a very nasty incidence of sexual abuse, which was repeated over a period of time. You can see how the imagery of the dream symbolically discloses her feelings of being a 'pawn' in a game in which she has no say, nor any power. She withdraws into soundless isolation, no one is there to take her part. As is often the case it is too dangerous to acknowledge the faces of these figures who can toss her about so casually. She is completely at their mercy and at any moment may be indifferently 'dropped' to her destruction.

Children who have explicit dreams involving a repetition of the sexual activity that constitutes the abuse, will very rarely describe such dreams unless they have found a safe, nonjudgemental environment in which to do so. Threats from the abuser should the 'secret' be revealed cause such dreams to be feared and censored to the outside world. And children for years have been disbelieved when they spoke of abuse. Since Freud's rejection of his first findings on the high incidence of sexual abuse, when he chose to view the experiences revealed to him as fantasy rather than fact, a legacy of disbelief has been the lot of too many children. It is vital now that we do not betray children again by denying the terrible problems of their abuse.

Maureen (15) comes from a home where she suffered abuse. Her father does not now live with her and her two brothers, but scars are still there for Maureen and she still feels very mixed up about her mother. She has been treated as an out-patient at a children's psychiatric unit; one of her disturbing, recurring dreams provided much insight into her complex feelings of need and hate of her mother, who never actually managed to protect her from the abuse:

> Me and my mum and sister are travelling in a car on a road. My mum is in the passenger seat. She has this knife. She stabs my dad who is driving. The car stops and she gets out. She runs in the field next to the road. I run after her. Suddenly, I have a brick in my hand. My mum stops and turns around. I throw the brick at her. It doesn't hit her, it goes through her. She falls to the ground, then I wake up.

The 'insubstantial' mother in this dream at last turns on Maureen's father. But Maureen's pent-up anger must have a further release, which it does when she throws the brick. As in any 'car dream' it is important to know who is in the driving-seat; it reveals a lot about who the dreamer sees as being in control. Maureen saw her father as the 'driver', the one in control who for years dominated the whole family.

Terminal illness

Although I personally did not collect dream data from terminally ill children there has been much work done in this area. Elisabeth Kübler-Ross found that on the whole children do know what is happening to them and go through the same common grieving patterns that adults experience, though not necessarily in the same sequence: denial, anger, bargaining, depression and accept-ance. Acceptance involves an awareness of the situation and a determination to live life to its fullest in their remaining days. Fear will also be very much at the forefront of a child's experi-ence of facing death, and dreams may well reflect their deepest anxieties. Kübler-Ross found that children symbolically express their knowledge of death to those who will hear them. Thus it becomes of vital importance that you listen to the dreams that terminally ill children try to tell you. They need to be heard.

In terminal illness, patients often dream of death when others may be trying to keep the truth about their condition from them. They may dream of the length of time before death. However, it is important to recognize that dreams of death in the healthy or slightly ill person are much more to do with the expression of fears about dying or about the 'death' of one aspect of life and the 'birth' of another. For instance, many adults dream of the death of a partner around the time of divorce, such dreams reflecting emotional changes rather than physical death.

As J. Bertoia and J. Allan have found, the unconscious is often expressed by children in spontaneous drawings and ther-apists using such drawings are highly trained and aware of the dangers of projecting personal ideas on to what they see. Always the consideration is, 'What is the child expressing here? And, how does it make me feel?' The inner struggles are very often expressed on a symbolic level before the child says them. Draw-ings made during art-therapy sessions, for example, can also be used as a basis of communication with the family. In such emotionally highly charged times, family members may need help in being with their child and talking to her, so fearful are they of saying and doing the wrong thing, and so devastated by their feelings of powerlessness. Dreams and drawings can be used as a vital bridge between the child and her parents.

Dreams prior to illness, during illness and following illness can help us to understand how our minds and bodies are working. They may reveal the way in which some of us have an underlying need for symptoms, a covert need to be ill in order to avoid stressful situations or in order to give ourselves a break from stressful lives. In neurotic and psychosomatic illnesses, which are as debilitating and painful as organic illnesses, self-enlightenment is equivalent to healing. Learning about dreams can help both children and adults develop insightful, health-promoting self-awareness.

SIX

Psychic Phenomena and Dreams

A long history of psychic phenomena

Psychic phenomena (psi) has intrigued and baffled humankind for centuries. In 2000 BC the Egyptian papyrus of Deral-Madineh gave examples of divine revelation in dreams, and oracular dreams were considered when decisions were made about matters of state. The Egyptians even tried to communicate with others via dreams, perhaps an early recognition of telepathy, for they believed homeless spirits carried the message from one dreamer to another.

Most of the dreams that have been passed down from antiquity are prophetic, though a few are telepathic in nature. The word telepathy – from the Greek root *tele* meaning distant and *pathe* meaning feeling – was introduced in the nineteenth century by F. W. H. Myers. Noted dream researcher Van de Castle found about seventy references to dreams and visions in the Bible, while in ancient Vedic literature from the Orient, dreaming was regarded as an intermediate state between this world and the next. According to B. Wolman's *Handbook of Dreams: Research, Theories and Applications*, it was believed that the 'soul' could roam in space and see this world and the other.

Aristotle and Democritus, *c*. 350 BC, both made paranormal dreams the subject of scientific inquiry and concluded that such dreams were transmitted by a sender to a receiver (dreamer) through atoms or by waves transmitted through the still night air, in much the same way as a stone sends out ripples when dropped in calm water. Democritus realized that the emotional state of the agent or sender of the message was very important, since images projected by someone in an agitated condition were thought to be especially vivid. This recognition of the highly charged emotional state of the sender is a view reflected in current anecdotal and experimental evidence which we will look at later.

In 1882 the British Society for Psychical Research was set up, and dream telepathy became a subject of considered scientific investigation. In 1886 three of its founders published *Phantasms of the Living*, a classic study of the paranormal. It quotes 149 examples of dream telepathy which had been rigorously examined and verified by strict standards, and while not all these dreams would meet present standards of modern investigative criteria, a great many would. The characteristics of the telepathic dreams and their 'causes' are in keeping with what children told me about their 'strange' dreams.

Today there are many reported incidences of telepathy, precognition, clairvoyance and other forms of psi or Extra-Sensory Perception (ESP). The terms psi and ESP include experiences which are sometimes referred to as paranormal, but which include telepathy, precognition, clairvoyance and other related phenomena. Although ESP is contrary to the laws of nature – according to the scientific establishment – we now know that nuclear particles communicate with each other in ways which show that those 'laws' do not explain the whole picture. Physicist Danah Zohar, in her book *Through the Time Barrier*, shows how in quantum mechanics, particles appear to be able to respond to each other instantly even though separated by enormous distances. Atomic and sub-atomic science may yet provide clues to the mechanism behind psi phenomena.

Children may learn about psychic matters through television programmes, newspapers, books and general conversation but they also learn through personal experience. In my research for this book I did not directly ask about dreams and psychic phenomena, partly because I wanted the questionnaire to be simple enough for children to complete on their own without having to include lengthy explanations about psi phenomena, and partly because I wanted to see if children would spontaneously report such dreams. They did.

Your own experiences will influence your reaction to this aspect of dreams, as will your openness to new data on the subject. However, as with all other dreams, listening to and respecting children's experiences in their dream life is as important in this area as it is in any other. Psi phenomena in children's dreams is not rare. In a study undertaken by J. Prasad and I. Stevenson of 900 Indian school children, 52 per cent reported experiencing it in their dreams.

Aloysius (11) recounted a psi dream:

> Just one week before my grandma died I had a very strange dream. I dreamt that I was walking down the backs of some houses and I found a memory card of a man. I picked it up, carried on walking and came to a back garden. In this back garden there was my grandma with a tall dark man in a black cloak and a black hat. They were at a man's wake and it was the same man as in the memory card. The next week my grandma died. She had a wake and I was given a memory card of her.

He felt his dream told of impending death, but he did not associate it with his grandmother's death, even though she was the only person in his dream that he knew. The inclusion of a wake and memorial cards reinforce the death imagery. Aloysius's grandmother was Irish, and in his dream all the trappings are linked to her culture. If he had dreamt outright that she had died, the dream may have been too disturbing for him, so it is the theme that is clear. We will examine precognitive dreams in detail later in this chapter.

Can you inherit dreams?

'My father and daughter speak in their sleep. Does this run in families?' asked Joyce. 'What hereditary traits are there in our dream lives?' asked Marina (14), who also told me that both she and her mother seem to be able to dream each other's future about two years ahead, and that her grandmother was similarly gifted. One reason for such similarities may be a genetic factor which the family members share. However, it may be simply because in some families it is permissible to talk about such dreams and so they are revealed. Many adults and children alike have said to me, when commenting on a dream that they regard as psychic, 'Please don't think I'm mad', or, 'I'm really a sensible person, not weird or anything.' The taboo around psychic phenomena is still very strong, for although witches are not now burnt at the stake for their inexplicable intuitions and prophetic dreams, there is still a climate of dismissive condemnation to be found.

Marisa, a mature psychology student, told me of dreams that she and her children share:

If ever I was unwell or had a temperature, I used to have a sensation dream – that's the only way I can describe it. My children have the same thing and although they try by using the same metaphors as I did, they too cannot explain it properly. It's as if you are getting bigger and bigger; you're a marble or something that is moving towards a 'hole', and yet it is not a hole, it's a sensation of something that might engulf you, except it never does. Your hands are big and heavy and your body leaden, yet you roll!

Marisa was still very perplexed about the dream and found information contained in Chapter 5, Childhood Illness and Dreams, helpful. But did her children inherit the dream or had they unconsciously stored information given by her when she talked of the dream and then believed it to be their own? A similar thing can happen with photographs from childhood; sometimes it is difficult to know if we really remember the holiday or just the image in the photo! With the dream Marisa and her children share, much will depend on whether they knew of it prior to their dreams.

Sarah, a medium from Liverpool, was surprised to learn, when encouraged to find out if any of her children had psychic experiences, that her granddaughter had often had dreams which

Vivienne (*13*)

either foretold or happened at the same time as certain events. For instance, she dreamt of a bus crashing into a local crowd waiting at a bus stop just before it happened, and another time she dreamt of illness within the family which came to pass a few weeks afterwards. Sarah said, 'I just never knew because we never talked about dreams. Now I'm going to contact the rest of the family to ask them.' Inherited abilities skipping a generation maybe?

In my work on dreams. I have come across innumerable examples of dreams in which the dreamer has been very concerned about another member of their family, so much so that they have contacted the person on waking to find out if everything is alright. For example, Gaynor dreamt of her sister crying out. On phoning her sister next day, she was told that her sister had had a terrible nightmare in which she had been screaming and calling out. On several occasions Gaynor and her husband have had identical dreams on the same night. We will consider this in more detail later in this chapter.

Lucid dreaming

Lucid dreaming is different from ordinary dreaming in that the dreamer knows he is dreaming while still in the REM state. Out of this awareness comes the ability to control the dreams. He can direct the action, choose what happens in the dream and take off – often into flying dreams.

Celia Green, Director of the Institute of Psycho-Physical Research in Oxford, first coined the term 'lucid dreams', though it is not a new phenomenon. A nineteenth-century nobleman, the Marquis Hervey St Denis, published the classic *Dreams and How to Guide Them*, which was all about dream control. Other cultures advocate the use of lucid dreaming; Tibetans practise a kind of dream yoga which involves lucidity; Innuit people use controlled dreaming for divination and healing, and in Malaya there are dream schools where children learn how to conquer their night-time fears. The Senoi, as this group of people are known, offer us great insight into the world of dreams, as we shall shortly see.

The ability to control dreams often begins in childhood, as it did for Jane, who came on one of my management training courses. She remarked that she was able to control her dreams more then than she can now. She regularly had pleasant dreams, woke from them and then returned to sleep to continue them. Some children have a brief snatch of lucidity in disturbing dreams where, still in the dream, they say to themselves, 'It's only a dream, I can wake up,' and they do wake themselves up.

Recent research into lucid dreaming has been carried out at St Thomas' hospital, London, by Dr Peter Fenwick and Dr Morton Shatzman. Their subject, Alan Worsley, has been keeping a diary of lucid dreams since his teens. Now in this forties he has helped to show that lucid dreamers can communicate to observers while still in the dream state. For the first time, Dr Fenwick argues, dreamers may be able to tell us their dreams even while they are having them.

One way of testing whether you are in a lucid dream is to try to turn on a light while still in the dream. Keith Hearne, inventor of 'The Dream Machine' which aims to test lucidity, found in his experiments with dreamers that, having previously been instructed to find a light and turn it on in their next lucid dream, they were unable to do so. Sometimes the light switch did not work or they could not find it. In one case the light could not be switched on until the dreamer closed her eyes. All this points to the idea that there may be an optimum level of light in lucid dreams. Maria (15) remembered dreams she had at about 10 years of age in which she knew she was dreaming.

> It was dark so I wanted to switch on the light on the stairs . . . I tried to flick the switch but found it was squashy and rubbery and impossible to operate.

Dr Hearne sees such machines being used in the treatment of nightmares. People could be wired up to the machine and when entering a nightmare, they could signal the information to the machine and be woken by a pre-set device. However, the main drawback that I see is that this treats the symptom and not the cause. It is much more important to find the source of the nightmare and deal with that, rather than manipulating the symptoms. Perhaps we need to return to the principles the Senoi used in their dream-work to discover how such an approach might work.

Senoi

The Senoi Indians of Malaysia practise and develop dream control as part of their culture. Their peaceful community owes much to the fact that from the earliest possible age children are encouraged to speak about their dreams and pay heed to them. If the child experiences fear in a dream he is asked to describe it, to speak of the fearsome animal or monster and to act out the dream. Members of his family and friends take on roles and ways are found which could help the young person deal with the frightening situation. He is then encouraged to confront the danger should it appear in his next dream. The basic principle is that if he confronts danger in his dream life he will overcome it in his waking life.

The Senoi recognized the importance of acknowledging and facing our fears. Modern de-sensitization programmes are based on the idea of facing fears and gradually building up skills which empower the individual and reduce or eradicate the phobia from which he suffers. There are no taboo areas in the Senoi dream tradition; children are taught to consider all dream content and to seek the meaning held in their dreams. Older members of the tribe would look for signs that the child was becoming empowered in his dreams, mirroring and encouraging the rise in personal autonomy and self-reliance in waking life. As Patricia Garfield, an American dream researcher, tells us in *Creative Dreaming*, by the time of adolescence a Senoi youngster does not have nightmares. He is regarded as immature until his dream characters assist him; when his dreams are positive, he is considered a man.

Astral projection and OOBE (Out-Of-Body experiences)

When I asked young people what information they would like to have included in this book, Poppy (14) said:

> I am totally fascinated by the astral plane and dreams about it. The prospect of the soul leaving your body during sleep is amazing. Maybe you could find out about a child's experience on the astral plane.

An 'out-of-the-body' experience is one in which a person feels he perceives the world from a location outside his physical body. There is a strong relationship between having OOB experiences and frequency of dream recall, lucid dreams and flying dreams. The same people tend to report all three types of experiences and recall their dreams more readily. Maria (15), whose lucid dreams we've already come across, provides an example of this; as a prolific dream recaller, she also has dreams which may be considered precognitive:

> This may sound strange but sometimes I have a quick snatch of a dream, it may be an object or something that will happen to me and it does. When it happens I think, 'Hold on, I've seen this somewhere before.

Vivienne (13) told me about her first OOB experience in a dream. It carries a number of familiar hallmarks, such as the rising above the body and looking down, and the shaking or jolting associated with the return to the physical body:

> I was in hospital and the doctors were operating on me and my spirit rose right out of my body and my spirit was looking right down on me. My body was dead but my spirit was alive trying to wake my body up and when my spirit returned to my body I felt the bed shake and woke up.

Dreamers report difficulty sometimes in getting back into their physical body, or a disinclination to do so. Often they remark that a voice or person may tell them it is not yet time for them to leave their physical body. Such events begin in childhood but are often repressed or kept secret for fear of ridicule or disbelief.

Matthew (12) when he is ill dreams that he floats to the ceiling as if he is a ghost. The experience of being separated from one's body is recorded in the Bible, where in Ecclesiastes 12 a 'silver cord' attaches the astral body to the physical body, lest the spirit or soul become lost. Children report astral travel or OOB experiences while awake or under anaesthetic as well as during dreaming.

Dee, now 25, told me that since childhood she has had precognitive and OOB experiences in dreams. She remembered being chased, gasping for air, dreaming and yet knowing that she had to get back to her body. She was afraid to discuss this with anyone because she felt no one would listen to her. Nearly all of what she dreamt came true she said, which made her not want to dream; she thought there was something wrong with her. However, as she has got older she has learnt to accept and use her unusual insights.

Marisa, the psychology student we also met at the beginning of the chapter, recalled a dream she had when she was 13 in which she was killed in a car crash:

> The car was on a bend when the crash happened. I don't remember us hitting anything, only the sensation of being out

of my body and soaring upwards and of knowing I was dead and wondering where to go. There was no pain and no panic.

Aileen Cooke, *Out of the Mouths of Babes*, reports numerous cases of children who have had both waking and sleeping psychic experiences. She tells of children, having travelled 'on the astral plane', each returning to their physical body with regret because, apart from not wanting to leave the beautiful world they discovered, they did not wish to take on the cumbersome burden that their body had now become. Others report flying through the air to see people and places, and being able next day to relate what was taking place far from their home, events about which they could not otherwise have known.

Synchronicity

Jung, who had many psychic experiences in his life, put forward the theory of synchronicity to explain the nature of 'meaningful coincidences'. These have an element of surprise and wonder for us; out of the blue a number of events happen together, and though unplanned they seem oddly linked and significant. Frequently they prompt us to some action or decision. Jung tells us to note these 'coincidences' or synchronous happenings because they act as signs to tell us about the road we are on and the direction our lives are taking. When synchronicity strikes, and events follow a dream, we may say that the dream is precognitive.

Children are sometimes quite disturbed by psi phenomena in dreams, yet in waking life people may almost take it for granted, as when a friend calls and we say, 'Oh, I was just going to ring you'. If a child can learn to appreciate that synchronicity is an everyday occurrence for the majority of people in the world, then he can note such events and see that they need not be frightening at all but indeed may be very important in making decisions. For instance, Kirk (14), when involved in choosing options for examination courses, wanted to do chemistry but he

Charles (6) Monsters and wild animals regularly chase Charles in his dreams. He cannot recall a happy dream and no one has ever listened to him when he spoke of them. Notice how even the sun is unhappy.

loathed the teacher so much that he was going to drop the subject. He had a week left before the choice had to be made. However, he had a vivid dream in which he was working in a laboratory and really enjoying it. Then a few days later he saw a careers film which pointed out that he would have to do chemistry if he wanted to follow his now chosen path. Shortly afterwards the best piece of synchronicity happened as far as he was concerned. His class was told that 'Mr Loathed', the chemistry teacher, would not be taking them for the examination course because he was taking up a new appointment elsewhere. Kirk felt free to opt for his desired subject – synchronicity! If children recognize this in waking life it becomes less difficult to accept should it happen during dreaming.

In 1962 a dream laboratory was set up at Maimonides Medical Centre in Brooklyn to investigate dreams and psychic phenomena. Since then hundreds of experiments have been carried out under the direction of psychoanalyst Dr Montague Ullman and others. What is fascinating about much of the research is that under rigorous scientific conditions, many experiments were significantly successful, particularly those involving dream telepathy, backing up evidence from other sources that extra-sensory phenomena occur during the dreaming state.

Precognition

Precognitive dreams are those which concern an event that has not yet occurred. The dreamer may know that whatever it is will happen in the future, or may awake thinking that the dream was bizarre, odd or of special significance. Some precognitive dreamers comment that the quality of the precognitive dream, perhaps because of its vividness or a peculiar light quality, sets it aside from their ordinary dreams. Others have learnt that their dreams are precognitive or telepathic only after they have been recording dreams over time; looking back at diary entries they see the links between their dreams and waking events.

Kathryn (17), now studying for her A-levels, has been keeping a dream diary for four years, ever since she began to realize that her vivid dreams were telling her what was going to happen. She said:

> During my late teens I've had some very strange experiences in my dreams. There have been two occasions on which I've been able to control events in my dreams and at both times the same thought has occurred to me – 'This is only a dream I could fly if I wanted to.' So I fly for a while, but unless I concentrate I lose control.

From lucid dreaming and flying she discovered precognitive dreams. The most startling one she found was about the accident at Chernobyl. A drawing illustrated her dream report:

> All I knew was that the building in my dream was a nuclear power station and that it would catch fire. It was as if this scene in my drawing had intruded on another dream I'd been having, for I was walking along a motorway when I leaned on the barrier and saw the power station. I knew it was going to catch fire . . .

I noticed the power station was set on an island in the middle of a huge lake. I could see the far shore but it was a great distance away and on it there were fir trees. To my left was something that looked like a jetty or large pipe, it stretched across the water but did not quite reach the other side.

Then the power station caught fire, but silently. I didn't hear a sound the whole time I was watching. The fire grew very bright and as it faded, a kind of black snow started to drop from the sky covering everything.

Kathryn heard about the terrible Chernobyl disaster and thought how strange that she should have had her dream just at the time when the tragedy happened, but she thought no more about it. However, when she saw the televised pictures, the first thing that struck a chord was the tall spike on top of the building. Then she learnt that the power station was on a lake and that some of the reactors had caught fire. So many aspects seemed to tally. And the black snow – was that the radiation that so devastatingly fell? In her dream she had no idea where she was; she only recognized the place as she saw those first pictures on television.

Since this dream Kathryn has accepted that some of her dreams are precognitive and in fact has found them to be very helpful, as we will see later. Ian (14), on the other hand, is still puzzling about his dream:

One time I had a dream about me falling off our cabinet in the living room. About two months later my mate offered me a game of golf. I climbed on the cabinet to get a golf ball when my hand slipped and I fell. Then I realized that I had dreamt this and it had come true.

In recent years investigation into psi research has gained new impetus. Russell Targs and Keith Harary, in their book *The Mind Race*, report on current work in American and Russian research institutions, both civil and military. If these aspects of the psyche can be tapped and harnessed then communication satellites in space could become obsolete! Ten years ago fax machines were a fanciful dream, but today we use them to transmit visual material over hundreds of miles; magically it appears at its destination in minutes. How much more intricate and amazing is the human brain, and who knows what potential may yet be discovered, or perhaps rediscovered.

Fiona told me that when she was 16 she had a horrendous dream about a woman tottering alone, drunk and derelict. At 18 Fiona left home for London and became, as she said, 'a raving alcoholic' and lost her health within a matter of months. Though she has since recovered, she believes this dream was a warning she should have heeded.

Anna (10) has many dreams about future events, mainly trivial events concerning her family. She talks to her father about her dreams as, 'He is the only one that takes me seriously about my Forward-in-Time dreams.' As is often the case with psi dreams, the content is to do with minor family concerns but the intense quality of the dream is quite different from her other dreams.

Children's anxiety about psi dreams

Many children who have dreams which later come true, do not enjoy the experience. Rachel (9) put it very plainly:

I have dreams that come true and I don't like it.

Maxine (14):

One night I had a dream about walking down a street that I had never seen before. A few weeks later I was on the bus and I went past the street that I dreamt of and it felt really weird.

Perhaps the fear is because some children believe that we dream so that the dreams can tell us what will happen in the future. They worry, usually silently, that the dream events will come to pass. Wendy (14) shows her anxiety about this:

The most frightening dream for me is when I dream about

something and the next day or maybe in a week it happens to me or somebody else in that dream.

The best way to confront this anxiety is to assure children that though some people do have precognitive dreams, it is fairly unusual, and they can be very useful. Some people find such dreams helpful as they forewarn and forearm them. They act as an early-warning system.

One way to reassure the child is to ask him to keep a log of his dreams which he can then check against waking reality. Armed with noted dreams linked to subsequent events he will be in a position to know when and if his dreams really are of the psychic variety. Encourage him to honestly investigate, and do not dismiss what he says.

Hilary (11) told me that she dreamt of a flood in her home town of Strabane a few days before it happened; fortunately she was not harmed. But that was not so for Eryl. In 1966 Eryl Mai Jones (10) insisted that her mother listen to her dream, even though her mother said she was too busy. Eventually she gave way and Eryl told her that she had dreamt that something black came down over her school and covered it. She initially refused to go to school. However, in the end she did attend on that fateful day when, with 143 fellow pupils, the school in Aberfan was buried under black coal slag.

Eryl may have had an anxiety dream brought about by living in the shadow of the coal tip, but J. C. Barker, a consultant psychiatrist, who undertook a thorough survey of premonitions about the disaster, judged it and many other dreams to be genuinely precognitive. In fact, so impressed was Dr Barker by the number of premonitions, involving people living outside Wales as well as the local community, that he was instrumental in setting up a British Premonitions Bureau in 1967.

Delia, now 17, recalled her earliest precognitive dream. She said:

I was about 8 at the time and vividly remember a very disturbing dream in which my mother was screaming and there were several surgeons and lots of light in an operating theatre. I was watching but held away from her.

When Delia was 9 her mother had to have a hysterectomy and was in hospital for a long period during which her daughter was not allowed to visit. Delia added that, 'Since both my mother and I have precognitive dreams regularly it is discussed a lot in our home. It is not a taboo subject and is readily accepted by my parents and other relatives.'

Déjà vu

One variety of dream that may lead people to consider the validity of psi phenomena is when *déjà vu* arises; the feeling that 'I've been here before'. A large study of the general public reported by Peter Evans in the 1960s indicated that 80 per cent of those who took part had had the experience. And children reported such feelings of *déjà vu* to me. Fourteen-year-old Andrea is only one of many:

> One night I dreamt that I was going on a journey with my parents and family and in the dream we went into a shop. I could picture the whole shop and the shopkeeper. The next day we did go on a journey and we went in a shop and it was the same as in my dream. It was quite scary.

One of the explanations for this widespread phenomena is that of paramnesia – one side of the brain notes a scene a fraction before the other hemisphere, and 'invents' a memory of the dream in order to account for that 'I've-been-here-before' sensation. However, too many examples of dreams, recorded years before, tell us that such a simple explanation will not suffice. People have had dreams in childhood, but not until adulthood has the *déjà vu* experience occurred. They experience a setting, being with certain people, or know with certainty what words will be next spoken in the conversation, even though there may be many years between the dream and the *déjà vu* time. Look out for the number of people who say, 'You just broke my dream', or refer to it in some other way, when a dream they have had has been enacted in waking life.

Death

Dreams of the death of a member of our family may occur because subliminally we have recognized physical changes in that person. Where there has been no communication in the weeks prior to such a dream, it is much harder to explain how we can know of the death, especially when the time and details are so graphically incorporated in the dream.

Young children in particular may feel that if they dream of the death of someone, and it happens, they are responsible. When Rose, now an adult, was between 5 and 7 years old she used to dream about people before they died and saw their funerals. Many times her dreams proved to be correct and she firmly believed the deaths were her fault. Though the dreams stopped when she was 10 years old, she still continued to have flying and lucid dreams. Lucy (12) wrote:

> My grandfather was a very good sportsman. Two months before he died, I dreamt that my family and I were watching the regional news when there came a tribute to him on the TV. The tribute showed pictures of him playing football and other games, then at the end the presenter said, 'And that was a tribute to Robert Sidney W— who died today at the age of 87.'

The dream gave her space to think about her grandfather and tell him how much she cared for him before he died. Lucy also dreams about hearing from a friend who lives far away and receives letters the next day. She commented that the quality of light in these dreams is different from that in her 'ordinary' dreams.

Graham Greene at the age of 5 had a vivid dream of a disastrous shipwreck; he later discovered that the *Titanic* went down that night. In his book, *A Sort of Life*, he tells how important his dreams have been to him, including more that were either telepathic or precognitive, especially concerning disasters and death.

Toni-Marie (6) Ghosts and genii chase the frightened girl. She is crying and yelling because she wants them to stop.

Friends

Friends regularly star in children's dreams and in some cases the dreams are precognitive. When Helen (13) was 8 she dreamt that her best friend at school broke her leg. Four days later her friend was knocked down by a car and her leg was broken.

Lottie recalled an upsetting dream from her childhood in which her best friend was 'carried away' from her, while Lottie herself was held back. The next day her friend came to tell her that her parents had decided to emigrate to New Zealand. Perhaps Lottie on a subliminal level knew such a decision was imminent and had read the signs that this would be the outcome. Her dream symbolically portrays the emotional impact of losing her friend. Now an adult, Lottie has had many precognitive dreams and waking psychic experiences. Her first precognitive dream was when she was 10 years old:

> I saw my mother flying through the air like a seagull. She plunged into a pool laughing wildly and said, 'Here I am the Sunday cook, fallen into the pond.' When I told her of the dream, she said the cook had been called away to see a sick relation quite suddenly and Mother had to cope with the weekend household menu.

Michelle (11):

> When I dream about something it happens in real life a few
> days later. I dreamt my cousin fell off the swing in the park
> and he did. I dreamt about me and my friend going to
> Southport and the next day we went.

Of course, some of this can be explained easily; the child is
looking foward to an event already known about. It is anticipation rather than precognition, but other dreams are not so easily
explained.

Vicki (15) spoke of two dreams. In one her mother had an
accident and the sounds of police and ambulance sirens filled
the dream. Vicki was so disturbed by this that subsequently she
would cry if she heard a siren while awake. In another one, a
nightmare, she said:

> I was on holiday and eating in a restaurant when there was a
> loud bang and a man had jumped. Then I went on holiday in
> real life and it really happened.

No one had comforted Vicki with the fact that such dreams
have happened to other people throughout our recorded history,
and in many cultures people who have such dreams are regarded
as having special gifts to be developed, not hidden. If Vicki can
learn more about the nature of such dreams then she may well
feel less at the mercy of them.

Telepathy

Telepathy, the transmission of information from one person to
another, mind to mind, over distance, without using traditionally
recognized channels of communication, happens with adults and
children. Jung saw telepathic dreams not as supernatural but as
based on something inaccessible in our present state of knowledge. As we saw earlier such dreams occur at times of great
emotional unheaval, for instance at the time of death.

Perhaps it was synchronicity which brought Simon's mother
on to one of my courses. Though the course had nothing to do

with dreams, in the break she mentioned an odd dream that her son was concerned about. She said Simon (16) was worried that there was something wrong with him because of it. After we had talked it over, she went home able to reassure Simon that such dreams indicate a special kind of sensitivity and awareness and that far from being negative, he could learn to control and use such information in a positive way. At a later date I met Simon and he told me his dream for himself:

> I was dreaming an ordinary dream when suddenly it changed. I dreamt that someone on my mother's side of the family had been taken into hospital. I didn't know who it was but I knew the person was dead. Then I went back to my old dream. The middle dream was much more vivid. I told my mother in the morning because I still had an awful feeling. She had just got news that my uncle had died.

In a paper called 'Psychoanalysis and Telepathy', prepared in 1921 but not published until 1941, two years after his death, Freud conjectured that telepathy may be the original archaic method of communication used between individuals and as other sense organs have become more highly developed during our evolution, it has been pushed into the background. He put forward the view that such methods of communication could still manifest themselves under certain conditions. However, Wilhelm Stekel was perhaps the first psychoanalyst to observe that telepathic events happened between people bound by strong emotional links, a view supported by research at the Maimonides centre in the USA. Telepathic dreams have also been recorded between patient and analyst, a relationship where the 'therapeutic alliance' or bond is all important.

Retrocognition in dreams

Detailed historical-type dreams in children are defined by some as evidence of retrocognition, knowledge of time past, or a reincarnation from previous life. Aileen Cooke quotes the example of an 11-year-old girl who had a series of excruciating dreams in which she was held prisoner in the Tower of London and finally executed. The girl drew the axe from her dream – it was an unusual design – and asked to be taken to the Tower. There she found the axe, which was used for execution by beheading, to be of the same design as the one she had drawn. Now, whether this is an example of 'cryptonesia', where the dreamer has come across such information when awake but subsequently has forgotten it, or whether it is an example of retrocognition or reincarnation it is very hard to know. Many more examples are reported by the author for those interested in following up this aspect of dream life.

Steven (15) finds his dreams very useful since he believes they definitely enhance his memory. You can see he has an unusual facility in the dream-memory department:

> I have a lovely dream that jumps back all through my life. It memories all the happy things I have ever done and shows them in detail to me. My mind goes over them again and again. It does this so many times that my mind can remember anything ... The most frightening dream I ever had was when I dreamt I was going upstairs and suddenly everything changed into a ship. It was like the old emigration ships ... it seems so true.

Such dreams may prove to be uncannily accurate in details of clothing, surroundings, language; all the trappings of another era in fact. It may be that in these dreams the dreamer is of a different sex and of a different chronological age. It may be that the child has a dream life which seems to run parallel to their waking life, but which is set in a different era or place. Whatever the context such dreams are remarkably vivid to the dreamer.

Kathryn (17) has many, many dreams about the Soviet Union. Three dreams, which came in sequence, were centred on St Basil's Cathedral in Red Square. In the first dream she was going past St Basil's in a bus, in the second she was walking towards Red Square, and in the third she finally arrived and was looking up at it. Kathryn wonders if this series will come true for she has had precognitive dreams in the past. She also dreams of Gorbachev and of asking a Russian what life was like after a nuclear war. Does such a preponderance of dreams about the Soviet Union indicate a former life to which Kathryn now finds herself drawn back?

Touran (17), born and raised in the Middle East, told me of a dream she had when aged 5½ to 6 years old. It was of great importance to her at the time and has been ever since, so great was its impact:

I had gone to visit my mother's cousins with my parents. They had a beautiful old, rambling house with a wild garden. In a room I found a calendar on the wall and as I turned the leaves back, I saw pictures of people in different fashions. One picture that stood out in my mind was that of a lady in seventeenth-century clothes – large, decorated, wire-held skirts and tight bodices ... A wonderment grew in me and it was somehow impressed upon me that these were my ancestors, my family tree, my past.

She added that during the past few years she has become deeply interested in metaphysics and believes that this childhood dream shows past reincarnations: 'The picture I saw clearly could not be ancestors of this life for I was born in Iran, this time round, and such fashions have never occurred in Iran's history.'

Helpful psi dreams

After Kathryn (17), whose dream of the Chernobyl disaster was described earlier, accepted her psychic ability she had a very helpful dream:

I had another premonition the next year when I was 16. I attend the Girls' Brigade and every year we hold a rally at the Royal Albert Hall. Our district had put together a dance item with ribbons which we hoped to perform there, but first we had to be assessed ... Months before that happened I dreamt I was standing on the top gallery of the Royal Albert Hall reserved for performers and I was there because we had been accepted. After my experience with Chernobyl I accepted this as a possible premonition and it came true.

They were accepted and performed their item in 1987. Though she had never been backstage before, Kathryn found that the twisting corridors and staircase details and colours matched those in her dream.

Another way in which such dreams may be helpful is as preparation. Lorraine (13) said: 'I find dreams helpful because I sometimes dream of what is to happen in the future and then I refer back to what I did in my dream.' This is a view shared by Sally (13):

> One night I dreamt that I was taking part in an international dancing competition. I made it into the finals so I used my Grade-4 technique and they presented me with first prize and I woke up. The next weekend I won first prize in a dancing competition in London, so after all my dream came true.

She used the technique that had been so helpful in her dream!

Delia finds her lucid and psi dreams valuable because they allow her time to consider the event to come, whether it be a disagreement or a traumatic event in the family. Some dreams heighten her awareness of danger, warning her, and so she takes evasive action, finding ways of responding positively to the early insight to which she has been privy. Like other young people she found dreams of examination useful; they prepared her for questions that arose. Now 17, she still practises dream-control, even with precognitive dreams: 'In interesting precognitive dreams, I can wake up and go back to sleep and find out the outcome of what is going to happen.'

We need to take the psychic and spiritual experiences of children seriously, and treat their remarks with great sensitivity. Practical issues of daily living and socialization processes which decry psi phenomena may well smother ESP tendencies in children. As Montague Ullman says in *Working with Dreams*, 'We are not only able to scan backward in time and tap into our remote memory, but we are also able to scan forward in time and across space to tap into information outside our experience.'

By way of conclusion, when I was seeking out research material for this book in a major city library, I had to obtain special permission to examine *The Proceedings of The Society for Psychical Research*. On expressing surprise about this I was told. 'Well, that's all about witchcraft and that sort of thing, so we've got to keep an eye on it.' It was only the intervention of an assistant librarian who had attended a management training course run by me for the city council, and who vouched for my 'good character', that enabled me to use the material then and there. Otherwise, formal application and vetting would have been required entailing much delay. I include this story as an example of the way in which psychic phenomena, in dreams and otherwise, is still viewed with suspicion in many areas; not with healthy scepticism but as being akin to devil worship! Children pick up such notions and consequently may be, as we have seen, afraid of dreaming experiences they cannot explain. If we do not treat psi phenomena as a taboo area, wholesome open dialogue will ensue and we can help our children to make sense of both their inner and outer world.

SEVEN

Mangled by the Media

It is not just in the United Kingdom that there are grave concerns about the influence of media on children. Over 2,500 studies have been conducted in America into the effects of television violence on the behaviour of viewers. The overall evidence was strong enough to persuade the Surgeon General of the USA to issue a report stating that television violence is dangerous to young people's health.

That television has a significant influence on the lives of children, there can be no doubt. What hit me forcibly though, in doing this research, was the extent and depth to which videos and television are invading the psyches of our children; their dreams teem with images from the screen. In this chapter I will give examples of what I see as the invasion of the mind-snatchers and look at research evidence that should post a health warning in every TV and video shop in the country.

At a special conference on media research and education held in Switzerland, Miguel Reyes Torres asked a probing question: 'Imagine you come home from work and find a strange man talking to your 5- and 8-year-old children. Are you happy about this? Why don't we ask the same question when the kids turn on the TV? The symposium gave Torres, and other media educators in Latin America, an opportunity to describe how their culture and values are being eroded by the invasion of foreign culture via the television set. For instance, more than 50 per cent of television programmes in Chile are imported from the USA and it has been shown that parents there vastly underestimate the amount their children watch. Do you know what your child views on TV and how many hours a week she watches?

The vast majority of children who took part in my research dreamt about television characters and plots, though ages 8 and 14 showed peaks in which 84 per cent reported television-inspired dreams. Most were frightening dreams and nightmares. However, the influence of violent TV starts even earlier. In a survey carried out by headteachers, one nursery in five reported incidents of random violence. In June 1988 the Co-operative stores, a large retail outlet in the UK, began to withdraw 'toys of violence' as they termed them, banning many toys associated with popular television series. Neil Postman, professor of media ecology at New York University, also points out that Americans are exposed to 800 commercials each week and that as consumers they are heavily influenced by this. Their attitudes towards consumption are being changed, mainly encouraging greater materialism and self-interest. Do you find that your children are influenced by television advertising? Their dreams are; cuddly toys, pop star accessories and 'flavour-of-the-month' sweets all appear in their dreams.

Nightmare viewing

The pervasive influence of TV, videos and films is all too evident in children's nightmares. When disturbing films are seen before sleep then there is a greater proportion of anxiety elements during REM sleep. One 10-year-old boy in all innocence grasped the confusion between the nightmare as dreamt and the vision on TV. When asked why he thought we dream, he replied, 'Because we watch television with a nightmare on.'

Very young children are greatly affected by material meant for adults, and even though they may at first object or show signs of distress, parents often ignore them. They do not protect their child from that which may be overwhelming. Kane (6) has recurring nightmares about:

> ... video dead ... an electric saw. They sawed the monster's head off and then the monster got up and picked it up.

This is a straight replay of the video watched with his parents.

Now his dream life is contaminated with these overpowering images and he is afraid to go to sleep at night. His parents wonder what all the fuss is about and get angry with him. Kane is even more confused because he feels guilty that these films should upset him!

Repeatedly children articulated the sources of their nightmares. Martha (8): 'My dad gets a video out and I watch, then my nightmares are about the videos he gets out.' Pansy (12): 'I have nightmares every time I watch a film about ghosts or haunted houses. I sometimes wake up screaming or crying and my mum has to come in and calm me down.' Or we could consider Lisa's dreams; she too is 12: 'I have nightmares after I have watched a horror film. I go to bed and dream that someone is going to rape and attack me and then throw me on to the railway line . . .'

Four years before writing this book, when I was working on *Women Dreaming*, I had a letter from a very worried mother:

My son is 6½-years-old and has for the past three months been having nightmares about a man with no face, but a lot of hair, who slashes at my son with his fingers and cuts him all over. My son then wakes up in tears, very, very upset and absolutely terrified. This man is very real to him.

She was so worried that she contacted her son's doctor and teacher, who, in turn, spoke to her son, reassuring him that such a man was not real. Both professionals assured the mother that there was nothing wrong with her little boy; but, she asked, 'What could possibly cause such dreams?' Had she asked some of her son's peers maybe they would have told her about Freddy, a very 'real' character known to many.

Again and again I found myself faced with this horrendous figure; children saw him attack, felt his gouging fingers and heard his words, and his scraping nails. Celia (11) gave a typical example:

The most frightening dream I have ever had was all about Freddy Kreuger. I dreamt that when I was sleeping he came to me. His nails were big sharp blades and he was all burned. When I was sleeping he ripped my tummy open and ripped out my eyes. Then he took me to his house. It was full of parts of children which he had killed. Soon on in the dream he was going to eat me and all of a sudden I fell out of bed.

Freddy Kreuger, razor-gloved star of the *A Nightmare on Elm Street* series, plays to packed cinema audiences in the USA and Great Britain. Videos are now available for home viewing which explains why such young children have seen and been affected by the film. The most recent one in early 1988 grossed $12.8 million in its first three days. Horror is big money. Freddy has become so well known that terms used by him, such as his cry of 'fresh flesh' when he sees a new victim, have passed into street parlance in America. Freddy murders teenagers in the series, yet they are the ones who pack the cinemas. You can now buy 'Freddy' look-alike dolls, complete with imitation razor nails and gruesome extras for just a few dollars more.

What is it about this vile creature Freddy that has so captured the psyches of the young? According to *Time* magazine it is because Freddy symbolizes what teenagers love to hate, their fathers! Part of the explanation lies in projection – that psychological phenomenon which allows us to put on to others, 'project', feelings which we find too uncomfortable to own. So the viewer sees a highly dramatic acting out of his inner, maybe subconscious, violence, lust or cruelty. A waking example of this was the way in which Hitler and the Nazi brotherhood, projected all their negative feelings on to the Jews. They were accused of being hungry for land, despoilers of the weak, cruel and untrustworthy and power crazy – all attributes that the Nazi regime displayed. Young people project their feelings out on to others, and part of the process of growing up is learning to recognize and deal with those bits of ourselves which frighten or shame us.

Children do expose themselves to fearful stimuli and by facing it learn to overcome it. That is a healthy thing to do. There is also an element of bravado – seeing horror movies proves you are 'macho', that you can take it. However, do we expose many of our young to too much, too soon and with too little opportunity to reflect on what it all means? Does watching blood-letting become addictive, as junk food does?

Valerie Yule, a child psychologist working with disturbed children, found that as well as having a traumatic family history, most 7- and 8-year-olds had been constantly exposed to destruction and meaninglessness on television, without having the language to comprehend it. They were bombarded by violence but there was no rhyme nor reason to it; violence for them was just an ordinary, accepted part of life.

Horror movies such as *A Nightmare on Elm Street*, with gratuitous, mindless violence and exploitation of the weak, coarsen our attitude to life itself and blunt our senses. Such brutalization of the senses happens early. Has it begun for Robbie (9) who had a nightmare in which a man got an axe and chopped up a woman? It was inspired by the film, *Little Shop of Horrors*. His attitude to women has been coloured; he sees women as weak victims.

Many authors such as Edgar Allen Poe, and film makers such as Alfred Hitchcock and Ingmar Bergman, have frightened their audiences for years with their nightmare productions, which at times create a fantastic dream world. It is interesting to note that Poe, Hitchcock and Bergman all suffered severe trauma in childhood and the sense of being overwhelmed and powerless in the face of trauma is transmitted in their film imagery. As psychiatrist Christian Guilleminault says, 'The audience accepts the helpless panic and goes to bed to dream its bad dreams. Horror is contagious. It can be experienced by those who never themselves were directly horrified.' Children need not see the offending films themselves; others may tell them, spread the contagion of fear, and as if by proxy the dreams occur, as in the case of the $6\frac{1}{2}$-year-old I mentioned earlier.

Guilleminault also points out that films, TV and books may reactivate past traumas or stresses, making the individual attempt to face them once again. This, of course, is perfectly acceptable for adults who actively choose what they watch, but it is another matter entirely when children are subject to material they cannot evade. They may have old fears evoked with no help to deal with them; just reactivation, never clarification and completion.

Some parents argue that none of this matters, that a child can leave the room if she does not like what is on the television screen. However, they overlook the need young people have to be with others. Young children want to be with their parents and so stay in what is usually the 'living room' of the house and they watch. What do they watch? A sample from 7-year-olds will give you an idea: *The Fly, The Day of the Dead, Jaws, Dracula, Rambo, Teen Wolf II* – the list seems endless. We

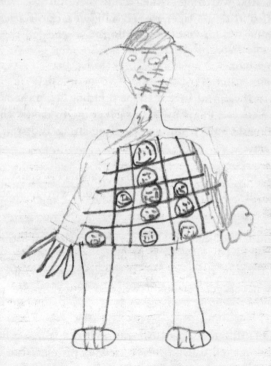

Ivan (10) 'I dream about this man with a dirty black hat and a ripped jumper and a burnt face and he kills children to get his powers.' – Freddy strikes again!

should also remember that children are heavily influenced by television advertising. Those of you with children will surely have heard the cry, 'Can I have one?' as the captivating toy appears in the commercial break. Children respond to media pressure to buy certain merchandise or to adopt gender-specific or class-specific roles: hyped life-styles mean money for the sellers! Unconsciously they become victims of the exploitative mind invasion of commercial advertising and of the video-promotion world.

In the processing work that dreams must do, it is clear that they will include content seen on television generally, not just video or television 'nasties'. For instance, Jonathan (14) has nightmares after watching crime reconstructions on *Crimewatch*, Seth (12) dreamt that a tiger ripped half his face off after he had been watching *Wildlife on One*. Wilbur (16) revealed:

> After watching a film about some killer bees, I dreamt that me and my sister were the only two people left on the earth because of these and I used to keep hiding from them in bins, in the sewers etc. I saw my sister get stung to death, then after a great time I could feel myself getting stung and stung until I blacked out.

As children grow they learn to distinguish between what they view and what happens in the outside world. Robin (16) said:

> One nightmare I have is simply being shot at point-blank range because I have seen it in films and it worries me a lot because I know there are people who are capable of such things. I never get seriously worried but they are just bad dreams.

He knows the difference and can rationalize his fears; however, research findings tell us that heavy viewers of television violence believe that the level of violence in the world is much higher than given by actual statistics. Fictional television truth is accepted above factual evidence.

TV and aggression

Startling new research from the USA, Israel, Finland, Poland and Australia shows how at certain times during a child's development, extensive exposure to television violence promotes aggressive behaviour in the child. American psychologists L. R. Huesmann and L. D. Eron discovered that children between the ages of 6 to 11 fell in this critical age range and chillingly they concluded: '. . . aggressive habits that are established during this time are resistant to extinction and often persist into adulthood . . . More aggressive children watch more violence and that viewing seems to engender more aggression.' This applies particularly to children, especially boys, who have poorer academic skills. They watch TV violence more regularly, behave more aggressively, and believe that the violent programmes they watch depict life as it truly is.

Huesmann and Eron gathered data over twenty-two years, following 8-year-olds through to age 30. They concluded that childhood aggression learnt from violent TV shows interferes with later intellectual development and may actually diminish cognitive achievement in adulthood. Aggression interferes with academic success because it causes difficulties with peers and teachers alike, further alienating the young person who thus becomes more isolated and in turn watches more TV. A vicious circle can develop in which TV becomes the fix and the viewer becomes the addict. This reinforces the aggression, and new aggressive schemes or codes are learnt and stored. In conclusion they state:

For girls and boys, television violence viewing was significantly related to concurrent aggression and significantly predicted future changes in aggression. The strength of the relation depended as much on the regularity with which violence was viewed as on the seriousness of the violence. For boys the effect was exacerbated by the degree to which the boy identified with TV characters . . .

Easy aggressive solutions to problems of living are offered frequently in television and video programmes. If you don't like someone 'blow him away', that is kill him; even the language becomes dehumanized and devoid of emotion, reinforcing the notion that life is cheap. If you have a bad relationship, then get rid of the partner violently or just leave. Very little emphasis is placed on trying to work through problems or accepting compromises. The value system of 'I should have what I want at any cost' – the consumers' dogma – particularly influences children who habitually watch aggression being used to solve problems. Ultimately such ideals have the power to destroy any society based on mutual caring and respect, and while television is obviously not the only factor, it plays a very significant part in influencing the value system that children adopt.

Calvin (12), whose father is in the air force, remembers having his first nightmare when he was 8. It was inspired by the film *An American Werewolf in London*, and his most recent nightmare was about his sister cutting her leg up and eating it on sandwiches. He is a fairly low achiever at school, though a popular boy, and he is easily influenced by his peers. He spends most of his spare time partaking of an unremitting diet of videos and TV crime serials. His dreams continue to be video influenced and are full of maimings and attack.

There are social repercussions too. Violent television, while it serves an escapist function, provides vicarious identification with 'macho', aggressive role models. Insecure young people frequently identify with such 'heroes'. However, the ironic contrast between their own abilities and life-style and that which they view leads to increased dissatisfaction and unease: the viewer feels even more socially inadequate. By the time the average American child contemplates high school, she will have spent more time in front of the television set than in the classroom. By age 19, she will have seen 22,000 violent deaths on television. It seems that the image manufactured for the masses and mass communication may take over from interpersonal communication.

Fantasy

Fantasy has always been part and parcel of our lives, and it plays an important role in enabling us to accept and master such emotions as aggression. By reading comics and books and by watching some programmes or listening to the radio, children can explore their own imagination. Fantasy can be a very healthy outlet for angry, socially disapproved of thoughts; the problem arises when the books, films and video methodology take over. Children have to learn that while in fantasy a character like Popeye can be beaten and survive such hostility, similar actions in 'real life' will cause felt pain. Children have to learn to contain and control their own violence otherwise the tantrum-ridden, lego-throwing toddler may grow into a weapon-wielding adolescent. People who take machine-guns into quiet streets and fire them off indiscriminately have, in the depths of their disturbance, lost the boundary between reality and fantasy; they have been unable to learn psychologically healthy ways of living in the world.

Eight-year-old Jake has nightmares about being bitten by dogs and being attacked but just occasionally he dreams he is The Incredible Hulk and he just 'grows and grows'. Then he can get his own back on all the people who are horrible to him. The character he chooses to be in his dream life becomes a monster when he is outraged; his anger explodes into gigantic proportions. This mirrors Jake's inner anger for which he can find no positive outlet. He is a boy who has been subject to a violent home and is both physically and emotionally malnourished. His dreams speak volumes. He, like The Hulk, frequently is overwhelmed by his anger against those who torment him, and he has terrifying, undirected outbursts of temper in school which cause real problems for himself, his fellow pupils and the staff. If no acceptable way is found for him to express these tensions he will probably end up suspended from school.

One unfortunate factor about television fantasy as distinct from fantasy found in books is that television is a very passive activity for children. They sit and are fed by the moving image. They need not imagine the setting, the accent, the characters of the story; it is all done for them. Such passivity does little to stimulate children's minds and while there is a role for television as relaxation, we have, as we have already seen, reason to be vigilant. Not all television programmes are of the 'moving-wallpaper' variety, but many deliver to children a junk diet of uninspired, poor quality pap. Junk food may have its place in the child's diet but should it make up the bulk?

Soaps

Television, like anything else in this world, is not value free. Soap operas may mirror society or help shape it. Children are avid viewers of TV soap operas and their dreams carry a host of soap stars. They identify with the story-line or character that holds significance for them. We can see a certain amount of hero-worship in these dreams: the dreamers see their favoured 'stars', meet them and get close to them. For instance, Michael (11) frequently dreams of Len, a male character in *Neighbours*; he would like to be like Len when he grows up. Holly (16) dreamt:

> The doctor off *EastEnders* once took one of our school assemblies, except the school was 'Grange Hill' and instead of a hymn he played pop music.

I wonder if this is also a daytime fantasy during tedious school assemblies? Jayne (12) dreamt that she was getting married to Den Watts, a character from *EastEnders*. But 11-year-old Marisa goes the whole hog – in soap terms. She dreams that she is Joan Collins in *Dynasty*, and she gets lots of money; wish-fulfilment running wild.

Girls begin regular viewing of soaps sooner than boys, especially in the 6- to 8-year-old group, and by 13 to 14 years of age top-viewing marks are given to soaps and certain beer commercials. Perhaps it is just the reassuring regularity with which soaps appear day after day that captivates children; predictability lends itself to feelings of security. As well as the sheer escapism involved in viewing, there is some cold comfort in knowing that, even with all that money, *Dynasty* stars can have an awful time too.

Pansy (12) 'I only have nightmares when I watch scary movies.'

The romantic element is particularly seen in girls' dreams. Nancy (12) said:

> I dream that I go out with a boy out of *Grange Hill* and that I ride Black Beauty and I'm on *The Clothes Show*.

Her hobby is horse-riding so it's not surprising that here again the wish-fulfilment element of riding Black Beauty occurs.

Certain typical themes emerged in a study of the content of soap operas: the strong woman, the supporting role of the family and the significance of home roots, especially at times of crisis. Soaps provide alternative families for us to observe. The families in *Neighbours*, the most popular soap with teenagers in my survey, have crises and disagreements just like our own, and that can be very comforting for children and adults alike.

Such programmes also allow the young viewer to identify personal problems he may not be able to articulate; an actor tells it on the screen and somehow that problem is shared. June (15) told me:

> I once dreamt that I was related to a character out of *East-Enders*. She helped me to sort my life out and warned me of events to come.

June found the dream very reassuring. However, there is a danger that the actors' solution may not be appropriate for the dreamer. After all, these are fantasy characters, not real flesh and blood, even though some children have great difficulty in distinguishing between the two.

Computerized space age

Young people are influenced by the technological hardware and concepts of our age of mass communications. They see programmes about space, they watch exploratory shuttles on the news and many children use computers both at school and at home. This clearly affects their dreams. Ned (8):

> My most frightening dream was playing a computer game when an arm comes out of the screen and pulls me in. I get into a battle between the Zoids and Droids. Me and the Droids haven't got enough ammunition and the Zoids have got enough for ten armies. When I was shot at I thought I was really dead, but then I woke up.

Larry (13) has a recurring dream:

> I dream sometimes of being a living robot in an unknown galaxy, fighting for freedom ... The planet is like a future earth. It is a lively and buzzing planet. My name is Thunder-cracker and I fight against Rastan. Rastan has only half a face. He sends out evil forces to destroy the planet, but we always destroy them before they get anywhere close to total domination.
>
> I am always on the run from Zarbor, Rastan's commanding officer. I am trying to find these special domes scattered about

the universe. There are eight of them and they power a ship controlled by computer with the most powerful zynap blaster in the universe. Trotans are iron soldiers and I am always blowing them sky high, but I always get taken prisoner. Then there is a massive fight in which I break out and then I get the domes and the planet lives in peace.

Larry has other space dreams, one in particular where he is a scientist working for NASA on a secret project. Again he is the hero and, despite overwhelming danger, he wins through in the end. His positive self-confidence, a great asset in waking life, is mirrored in his dream state. He is also at that crucial adolescent separation stage, where he seeks autonomy from his parents and has to begin taking his independent place in the world. The dream symbolically reveals this process. Charlie (12) also wins through; 'We eventually destroy their (the Martians) base, with force of course. Then we are knighted and everybody worships us.'

Both boys see themselves as heroes and saviours. This is not the case for Donna (10), from Hertfordshire, who had this dream when she was 8:

> The most frightening dream I've had is when these aliens came to earth and pretended to be friendly. Then they attacked, killing everybody except me. Then one ate me. It started on my hand and slowly worked upwards and I couldn't stop it. The alien had pointed ears and small beady eyes in a head too big for its body.

She was, at that age, still dealing with fears of being overwhelmed, as the image of being devoured so often reveals. The Spock-like ears are reminiscent of the popular space fiction programme *Star Trek*, which Kate may well have found disturbing.

It is useful to remember that we do not have to see programmes or read about the subject ourselves; the spoken word can be equally impressive. Dilly (7) usually dreams of dragons and fairies, but she dreamt of being in a rocket that went to Venus and Pluto after her sister told her about a school trip to Jodrell Bank.

Everyone can be a star – wish-fulfilment

Judo green-belt Barry (13), from Widnes, is overjoyed by his television-influenced dreams, for they are pure wish-fulfilment:

> I am part of a comedy act like Smith and Jones, and we are world famous and always doing charity shows to help people. We were going round clubs and being on TV and all the time we were getting richer and richer.

Success, fame, money and good works to boot! With Dora (14) it is slightly different: 'I have an acting position in *Neighbours*. I come out from working in the studios and everyone asks for my autograph.' Zachary (11) takes on the role of his hero. He told me: 'I dream about Spiderman and I am him. I have Spidersense and soldiers chase me.' Janine (16) used to dream of Spiderman too, except that she regularly helped him save people. She also received some of his ability.

Jenny (15) dreams frequently of Elvis Presley, and really enjoys her dreams because she always features as his wife. Craig (15) becomes a sports commentator in his dreams. Other adolescents dream of being with their favourite sports or television star, but in the dreams they are good friends.

Many young children, like 7-year-old Natasha, dream of favourite toys or meeting fairies and good goblins. Karen (11) dreams of Tom and Jerry, Bugs Bunny and Micky Mouse – cartoon characters are very well represented in children's dreams. Leonie wants all her family with her, so in her media-influenced dreams, all her family are cartoon characters!

Older children dream of current, chart-topping singers and groups. As does Rhona (14): 'I dream of TV characters and pop stars like Bros, A-Ha and Wet Wet Wet.' The video pop market available to young people filters through to their dreams where they happily recall their heroes. Jennifer (9) likes to watch pop-music programmes and dreams her ultimate wish:

> I grow up to be a pop star and have lots of beautiful horses and have lovely stables for them, and I have a lovely house for

my mum and sister and dad – and that my dad came back to live with us.

Influenced by books

Dr Johnson said that there were only two purposes for reading books; the better to help people to enjoy life or the better to endure it. In books we may find keys to understanding ourselves, our strengths and weaknesses. In reading to your own children, you can have an enjoyable time together in which you can experience all sorts of worlds and ideas. Recently I was reading *Stig of the Dump* to my 5-year-old daughter and she was fascinated but a bit frightened of the strange stone-age man who used all the cast-off bits and pieces of our society to build his home. One night after a dramatic high in which leopards chase Lou and Barny, the two children in the story, Crystal dreamt:

> Barny was outside in a mask and the leopard was there and Lou. And they were a little bit frightened. I was watching.

She was not too frightened, for, as you can see from her behaviour in the dream, she was detached and not threatened directly. We talked about how the children were safe with Stig and how he successfully got rid of the leopard, and reassured she fell back to sleep. However, this is a nice example of how emotions stirred up by the book are processed in the dream state.

Tracy (11) spoke for many when she said: 'I dream about books and I am the main character and play the most exciting parts.' *The Lion, the Witch and the Wardrobe* is a book that was frequently recalled as a dream stimulator, prior to it being televised as a children's series in Great Britain. Books like *The BFG*, by Roald Dahl, were also frequently mentioned by children who found their dreams responding to the vivid images and story lines of this highly popular author. Julie (12), a sporty girl from Kent, loves to read Dahl and finds her dreams influenced by the frightening and funny stories she devours: 'I had a dream once about *James and the Giant Peach*. I was a centipede.'

Zachary (11) Cartoon characters such as Spiderman are often featured in children's dreams

Jimmy (6), a partially sighted boy, dreams of being in the pages of his adored Mr Men books and playing with the characters. Similarly, Tracey (11) dreamt: 'about Starlight, the horse out of Rainbow Brite land, and Digby, the biggest dog in the world'. Tammy told me: 'I never have TV characters in my dreams but do have book characters, probably because I find books more captivating and read all the time. I still seem to get characters I liked when I was young.' They return her to an age when she felt sure and safe. The dreams leave her feeling warm and at one with the world.

Books inspire fantastic dream adventures. Jennifer (12), who enjoys American football and weight-lifting, dreams she finds Aragorn from *Lord of the Rings*; Helen (13) recalled dreams when she was younger where she became one of the Famous Five and went on adventures with them; while Yolanda (11) dreams that she is tomboy George, from the same series. She too takes part in wonderful escapades in a way impossible in her waking life.

Jeff (6), a serious, straight-faced young man, told me in great detail of his dreams of Moomintroll and his becoming the saviour of the Snork Maiden in his dreams. He added:

One day, in my dream, I was walking in Moominland when the Snork Maiden said, 'Why don't we go on an adventure?' 'Yes', I replied, then I went off.

His very advanced reading skills and problem-solving abilities reflected his high academic performance in school, and his written dream narratives were very detailed for someone of his age. However, the content is linked to family, for he, like the hero of this saga, is Nordic.

Not all books inspire pleasant dreams; other children dream of growing donkey ears after reading *Pinocchio* and wake touching their ears to see if they have really grown. Ahmed (9), son of a strict Muslim, had a nightmare triggered off by reading a ghost story. He was so scared that he woke up his sister who told him to pray and go back to sleep. However, he was still scared and started to cry but eventually got back to sleep. And Anthea (16) recalled a nightmare she had in which she was standing in front of a row of mummies' caskets. It was thundering and lightning and, suddenly, out of one of the caskets jumped Rupert the Bear, except he had huge fangs! Anthea said she could not sleep for many nights afterwards. This may have been induced by a Rupert story.

Books, however, can very often help children to understand what is happening in the world around them, as Grainne (11) tells us:

I once dreamt I was Karen in Judy Blume's book, *It's Not the End of the World*. This confused me but prepared me too. Karen's parents were splitting up and it shows what troubles they went through.

Judy Blume's collection of letters from children covers a whole range of issues that affect children, from divorce to wet dreams, and tells very straightforwardly what children would like to say to parents if only they would listen. The letters deal with those same tricky emotional issues that dreams reveal.

The following dream highlights the awareness that underlies many dreams. Kimberley (11):

> I once read a book called *Peter Pan* and I dreamed that Peter came and took me away to his land and told me I had to be his mother and do the washing and sewing and things. I wasn't allowed to go home so I don't like Peter Pan.

This seems to go to the heart of the underlying dynamics of some relationships women have with men. In fact Dan Kiley wrote a book called *The Peter Pan Syndrome* in which he argued that women fall for the perpetual 'little-boy' act that some men adopt and so women find themselves as surrogate mothers rather than wives. Kimberley did not need psychology books to explain this scenario – her dream made it self-evident.

Fairy stories

Fairy tales were the main source of entertainment for children for centuries and because television is such an insistent part of children's lives it is easy to forget that their fears existed before television was invented. One of the reasons fairy stories are so potent for children, as Bruno Bettelheim so lucidly explains, is because so many express the abandonment they feel in everyday situations; when they are left at nursery, when they are put to bed and told it's time for sleep yet they can hear the rest of the world going on round them, even when parents go out and a well-liked babysitter is left in charge. Feelings of being deserted may be quite powerful. However, working through such feelings, surviving them and feeling alright, can lead to liberation and independence. In such books as *The Water Babies* it is only after children have been left, lost or abandoned that things really start happening for them. They discover new worlds, new capabilities previously hidden from themselves, and begin to grasp the fact that they can separate from their parents and become autonomous.

Many fairy stories are violent and gory but the development and outcome of traditional stories make it easier for the child to understand the opposing forces of good and evil in a way most

Jake (8) More TV influenced dreams.

television does not. Additionally, when young children are being read stories they have the presence of an adult who will answer questions and share in the experience in a very direct way. The child can dictate the pace by stopping for explanations and the adult can screen out that which may be too strong for the child to deal with or too emotionally close to home or just be there to support her on a journey which may be difficult. Television affords little opportunity for such intimacy between parent and child, nor does it cater for individual emotional tailoring to your child's needs. Often watching television divides rather than unites families. As Ed Kittrell, Chief of the Department of Communications at the American Academy of Pediatrics said, 'A family watching television is alone with each other.' Children are told to 'shush' if they query what is happening, the speedy onset of dramatic highpoints in T V brooks no interference from puzzled or frightened children, especially as so much of it will be the 'after-nine-o'clock' material young children are not supposed to be viewing anyway.

Bettelheim, in *The Uses of Enchantment*, probably the most insightful book about fairy stories ever written, shows how important it is that children do not experience only pleasant, wish-fulfilling, happy fairy stories; a balance is needed. Children feel anger and hostility, violent emotion and feelings of helplessness; fairy stories enable them to realize they are not alone, that others have such feelings and that living involves a struggle between good and bad, fortune and misfortune and so on. Fairy tales appeal to both sides of reality and help children deal with their own deep, inner conflicts in a way much other children's literature does not.

As we have noted earlier, ultimately helping children manage their fears means helping them to realize they are not powerless victims, unable to affect change. Fairy tales show that the weak are not always overcome; wit and persistence, honesty and willingness to confront danger, albeit with a fast-beating heart, may still win the day. Parents can help the child by talking through fears at the once-removed position. You can talk about the feelings the fairy tale provokes, own some of those feelings as an adult, share your ideas with your child, tell her how as you get older you became less fearful or how you too still feel afraid of the dark sometimes. Communicate with children and let them know you empathize.

Comics

Sometimes comics like *The Beano* and *The Dandy*, to name two long-standing British classics, seem very violent, yet, as discussed earlier, part of the work of growing up is to master aggressive wishes. Hopefully children learn that feelings of violence and anger are normal but that they need to be channelled into socially acceptable behaviour. If a child fails to distinguish between acceptable expressions of anger and unacceptable forms, usually involving destruction of those around him, then he may develop serious emotional disturbance.

Shauna (11) orders a comic called *Nikki* and in it is a story called 'The Comp'; she dreams regularly of the twins Becky and Hayley, the stars of the story. Bangor-born Huw (10) dreams of Sooty, Garfield and also Tom and Jerry.

Throwing the switch

Morris (13) found his own way of throwing the switch on his bad dreams:

> When I was young I always used to 'nightmare' about things like skeletons or baddies, usually after watching a film. Now, however, I have taught myself to – before I go to sleep – think of nice things. My favourite one is holidays; villas in the Algarve, sun-blistered beaches in Spain, white waters in Canada . . .

Morris clearly has a very positive approach to nightmare reduction. Other ways are to consider what programmes your child watches and, if you are not sure, observe the child's reactions. You may be very surprised at what you see. If you have young children, watch with them rather than using the television as a third parent or an unpaid babysitter. Talk with your children about what they see, help them put it in a context of their own lives and their own world.

Just as we watch what food we feed our children because we know the harmful effects of certain foods and additives, so we need to look at the mental diet we feed them. We would not knowingly feed our children infected food which would cause them to be sick, yet many parents provide televised fodder which as the US Surgeon General said, is prejudicial to health.

EIGHT

Critical Life Events: Separation, Divorce and Death

As we have already seen, traumatic events affect the dreams of children and adolescents, just as they affect those of adults. Separation from loved ones, divorce, loss and death are part of a child's experience of life. It is to these that we now turn.

In Western society divorce is one of the most serious crises in contemporary life. In the last twenty years the divorce rate has increased 400 per cent; one in three marriages now ends in divorce. While most members of a divorced family ultimately cope with and come to terms with this critical life event, to quote J. Wallerstein and J. B. Kelly, there is no 'victimless divorce'. Frequently, we are surprised at just how painful separation and divorce can be and children's dreams at the various points in the process reflect deep anxieties.

Separation: what if my parents split up?

Hayley (14) contacted me about her fear-filled dreams of being chased. In vain she responded with futile slow-motion running on the spot. She also dreamt of being pushed off a cliff, falling and falling but never landing. She was worried about these dreams and said, 'My mum and dad are going through a shaky patch in their marriage and they argue a lot which upsets me. I go to school and because I am worrying I am grumpy and miserable. My friends are fed up with me and are not speaking to me. Do you think,' she asked, 'that I am having dreams like this because I am under quite a lot of pressure, as they seem to happen more recently?' Hayley answered her own question. Additionally she recognizes how her anxieties spill over into relationships outside the family, making her even more isolated and anxious. Her dream is remarkably similar to Jennifer's (9). Falling, a common motif in the dreams of children and adults alike, is the main theme of her dream. Jennifer recognized that her falling dream was provoked by her parents' struggle during a particularly violent pre-separation period. In the dream her father pushed Jennifer, her mother and her sister over the edge of a cliff; in waking life Jennifer feels she is going 'over the edge'. Life feels beyond her control and the dream reflects her belief that she has no secure ground left in her family life. When I asked her how she was feeling, she replied:

> It's hard with my family falling apart. Now my dad has gone and one of the best parts of my family, my nan, has died.

Her one solid landmark in the shifting ground was her constant, loving grandmother, always there, accepting and predictable. Her death was an additional loss Jennifer had to face.

Kerry (9), said her most frightening dream was:

> When I went to the fair and my mum and dad had an argument and my mum walked away and they had a divorce.

At the back of her mind was the niggling worry that her mother and father were on the verge of splitting up; no one had spoken of it, yet she could not bring herself to ask any direct questions in case she caused trouble and got blamed.

In the midst of parental conflict, children fear the break up of their home. They are anxious that they may have to choose, that they may be called upon to take sides and, worst of all, that somehow it is their fault that the relationship between their parents went wrong. Many children do blame themselves and develop strong guilt feelings which sometimes lead to disturbed and self-destructive behaviour.

Aaron (12) told me that he has 'great parents', whom he loves very much, yet he dreams of:

My parents splitting up and it is me who takes all the pain of who I want to go with and what would happen.

He is fortunate for he can talk to his parents about most of his frightening dreams and they are usually able to calm his nerves. But somehow this one, which expresses one of his worst fears, he cannot share with them.

Lovely dreams set in Crete, walking on sunny beaches with his parents, are the stuff of Spiro's (9) dreams. However, in stark contrast, he also has recurring nightmares of standing in court being asked to decide between them. Who will he live with? Overhearing late-night rows and fearing they will separate, he dreads having to choose. How can he? He loves them both so much.

It is clear from these dreams that children do worry about parents separating. Now, in response to such stress, there is more research going into conciliation and mediation processes. The results of a three-year study into ways divorcing couples were helped settle disputes over children, custody and access, as well as financial arrangements, show that the help of a neutral mediator was far preferable to slanging it out through lawyers in court. Apart from the saving in legal fees, families are helped to communicate with each other at a time when anger and resentment may make it otherwise impossible.

Some youngsters can take separation more in their stride. Indeed for some it may be a blessed relief. Steven (15) was frank in his comments:

I am an ambitious kid who is interested in many things, e.g. cycling, tropical-fish keeping, hi-fis, and windsurfing, who works his brains out trying to finance all these activities. Most of the time I'm knackered from working too much and I'm fairly happy although arguments between my splitting-up parents buggers me up a bit at times.

He dreams of being attacked by a bull but jumping aside at the last minute, being in the path of a speeding car, from which he is saved by waking up, but he added, 'I don't dream much because when I'm asleep, I sleep well, mainly because I don't get enough of it because I do three morning paper rounds and get up at 5.00 a.m.' But the dreams Steven does have reflect his concerns and indicate positive outcomes. You can see that in each dream he finds some means of avoiding catastrophe; though he feels threatened he is not overwhelmed.

Many children suffer greatly from lack of communication with parents who are in the throes of separation, and while it is understandable, since the parents themselves are going through intense emotional and financial upheaval, children need consistent support and need to know what is happening. They feel confused and unhappy because they do not understand what is happening or why, and no one is willing or able to explain the situation to them.

If you are involved in separating from or divorcing a partner you will find that talking to your children and answering their questions is ultimately the most constructive approach you can take. Even if you do not know what the outcome will be, you can prevent the building of fearful fantasies that the children resort to in order to fill yawning gaps in their knowledge. If a child has facts from you, and your ideas about what may happen in the future, he is less likely to assume that he will have the same experience as Jane down the road, who had a terrible time being used as a pawn in a game between her bitter parents.

Books can also help allay fears that result in disturbing dreams. In *Dinosaur's Divorce* by Laurie Krasny Brown and Marc Brown, the authors, both of whom have first-hand experience of divorce, present different aspects of divorce as seen through a child's eyes. Aimed at children of 10 years and under, it enables parents and children to share information and feelings through the vehicle of a beautifully depicted dinosaur community. A useful book-list resource, 'We Don't All Live With Mum and Dad', is published by the National Council of One Parent Families, 255 Kentish Town Road, London NW5 2LX. Libraries will also assist in the search for books which sensitively explore this area.

Moving out

If you listen to children talking about their dreams after one of their parents has moved out of the family home you may well become aware of aspects of the parting that are particularly stressful. Children are quick to realize that financial changes affect their new family unit and are aware of the strain this puts on the parents, particularly the mother, for she customarily is the person with whom the children live.

The father of Rhoda (10) left home a few months ago and her mother is running up a lot of debts. She cannot give Rhoda and her sister Kelly much emotional support as she has so many unmet emotional needs herself. There has been upset within the family for some time though, as you can see from Rhoda's comments:

> I dream about bad people coming to take me away. But my sister, Kelly, she dreams a lot of nightmares that get her sleep-walking. She sleep-walks outside. We both dream about men coming to take us away. We had the same dream on the same night.

When Rhoda was 'little', she said, lots of dreams came after watching horror films with her parents. Now that is not happening but in her dream life she continues to attempt to resolve the difficult family situation in which she found herself. She still feels that at any moment she may be 'removed' from home and there is no one to protect her or her sister.

Sally, a 13-year-old marching-band enthusiast, whose parents recently split up, often dreams about her 'dad being in the house on his own'. This upsets her. Not surprisingly her other dreams reflect anxiety about the separation. The worst one is where she dreams her parents are dying. She is so disturbed that afterwards she cannot go back to sleep. Her parents did not notice their daughter's disturbing dreams and her nervous behaviour because they were so preoccupied with their own conflicts.

In April I talked with 6-year-old Graham whose father had left the family only two weeks previously. His dreams were filled with fear and anger towards his mother. In one dream he sprinkled magic dust on his mother and she shrank and became stuck on one of the studs of his shoe. In another he saw his mother hanging on a cross, as in *Jesus of Nazareth*, the film he had watched over Easter, and when he looked up and saw her he cried. Was he projecting his feelings so that in fact he was the one who was being 'crucified' by his father who had forsaken him? Graham's other dreams involved shooting everyone or being chased by zombies and, hardest to bear, a terrifying nightmare in which his sister and mother disappeared.

Graham is not a highly disturbed child, in need of 'treatment'. He is still working well at school; he is still a popular outgoing boy and there are no overt signs of distress. However, these dreams allowed him to share the deep feelings of loss at his father's departure and his terror, unspoken, that his mother might go too. Having someone to talk to about his great anger and grief would help him adjust to his new living arrangements.

Graham (6) dreamt of his mother hanging on the cross. Unvoiced fears following his father's leaving home became mixed with the image of Christ's crucifixion.

And if someone was listening to his dreams, they would provide the perfect starting point for such discussion and support.

Divorce and after

Mavis Heatherington and colleagues reported in her paper 'The Aftermath of Divorce' that:

Our study and previous research show that a conflict-ridden intact family is more deleterious to family members than a stable home situation in which parents are divorced. Divorce is often a positive solution to destructive family functioning . . . it is important that parents and children be realistically prepared for the problems associated with divorce that they may encounter.

One common problem following divorce, which is rarely mentioned, is that many children experience very disturbing nightmares. Susie (6) has been having increasingly violent nightmares in which she brutally kills birds and animals. She awakes sobbing and screaming and re-experiences the distress when her mother tries to talk to her about the dreams during the day. At school she is sociable but never sticks up for herself if anyone hurts her or makes fun of her.

I asked her mother, Fiona, if Susie was able to express any anger in her waking life, since certainly there is a great deal expressed in the dream. But no, Susie is always controlled, never loses her temper, never argues back. She becomes distressed if voices are raised or if she witnesses an argument. She begs those involved to stop.

For Susie, loud voices and arguments recall the times before her parents separated. She links it to someone she loves leaving her and, like many children in similar situations, there is a fantasy that if she is very, very good, maybe that lost parent will return. Also she has a fear that her mother, who has been in hospital a number of times over the last few years, will also disappear so she must be a good girl to ensure that she will come back home. Therefore, while awake little Susie always tries to control herself lest her feelings cause problems; while asleep her defences come down and she cannot hide the intense anger.

These nightmares recur whenever Susie has witnessed a confrontation, however minor, and when she has been passive rather than assertive or aggressive. The dreams show that Susie needs to express her feelings. She needs time and patient reassurance in order to learn that her hostile feelings are permissible and that she will not be deserted if she expresses them.

Gwendolyn (15) told me that her earlier experiences have left their mark: 'I'm a very bad-tempered person and my life was hell. Since my mother and father split up I've been much happier and can control my temper as when my mum and dad were together they would fight a lot and my dad would then go out and get drunk.' She learnt the role of emotional care-taker at an early age; taking care of her mother's needs became of paramount importance. She also picked up an emotionally charged message that men are not to be trusted:

My most frightening dreams always have my mum in them and I always seem so protective with her. We are in life very close. In one dream my mum and I were on some swings and she had an accident where her nails started to pour with a liquid and I got so scared because if the liquid ran out you died. So I took my mum to hospital and I was the doctor. I helped my mum to get better and she didn't die.

While the symbolic life-blood flows from her mother, Gwendolyn has the enormous responsibility of reviving her mother and keeping her alive. Another of Gwendolyn's dreams makes this feeling of responsibility for her mother more understandable:

My happiest dream is of my brother, me and Mum being happy together. I never seem to want a father in any of my dreams because in real life I have a real dad who won't see me, a dad who adopted me and a new step-dad I don't get on with anyway, so they are never included in my dreams.

If I'm very good: getting back together

Obviously there will be many times when a child has an intense desire for her parents to reunite. And these dreams can be helpful for they give voice to the child's wishes. Acknowledging that wish and accepting the child's right to express it, however uncomfortable that may be for the adults, is important. Stephanie (13) provides an example:

> I dream that when my mum and dad broke up they would have just forgotten the past and just rewound back to where all the happy times were.

The yearnings for times pre-separation are clear. Stephanie needs to work through her feelings of grief and anger as well as guilt. She certainly feels rejected and jealous. She longs for the day when her father will show her and her twin sister more love. 'My sister and me wish he would just find some way of showing us he cared for us.' Now he has met another woman who has a son and daughter, which again upset Stephanie: 'I didn't like that at all because they made sure my dad loved them and took more care of them.' Her fear and anger can be seen in the following dream, her most frightening to date:

> This is what really did happen when my mum and dad broke up, and my mum, Rosie, came home drunk and tried to kill my dad. She had got him [with a knife] on the arm and back, then she got put in jail.

This dream was a replay of a waking event witnessed by Stephanie just before her parents broke up. She is still trying to come to terms with it and until she does so the dream will probably recur. Time to talk, grieve and deal with hurt is vital and if someone can support Stephanie through that experience, her dream will fade; the dream need not repeat once its message has been heard.

Not all children do want their parents to get back together, so, as ever, it is important to hear what children are actually saying rather than assume we know what they will say. Christina

(13) had a nightmare in which her mother and father, who are divorced, got back together, but then:

> My mum's second husband came along and killed him. Me and my brothers and sisters had to go in a home. I have dreams about my brother dying and my horse gets stolen and used for meat.

She added, if it is not already apparent, that she does not like her stepfather and in fact, refuses to call him 'Dad'. Notice from these dreams how she cannot keep hold of anything she cares for: her father dies, her siblings are taken away or killed and even her horse becomes merely dog food. She feels powerless, fearful that every emotional bond will be torn apart. No one, her dreams say, has any care and concern for her. No one is the champion of her interests. There is no one to act as an advocate for her while she feels so intensely vulnerable that her very existence seems to be threatened.

For Paula (12) there are no romantic images of the Father Christmas-like absent father who turns up once a week bearing gifts; she is happier living in a stable, loving single-parent household. She described her most frightening dream: 'My real dad came back and was going to take me away.' She fears being used in a game that her father might play with her mother; a game that is well known to professionals. The NSPCC 'Yo-Yo' study found that children are often used as pawns in matrimonial conflict and confusion may arise in the child who feels forced to reject, or protect, one parent in favour of another. We see the resultant anxiety in disturbing dreams, problem behaviour and poor school work.

Torn loyalties

Many children have dreams which feature the new partner of their parent. In some cases the child feels torn between liking the new partner but feeling that he is letting his 'missing' parent down. It may take years for children to get over those guilty feelings of torn loyalties. In other cases, the 'new partner' is well and truly detested.

Belinda (15) asked me to keep her real name secret in case her father found out what she had said to me. Both her dreams and her comments are highly informative. At the time of her parents' separation she used to dream about the world being blown up and only herself, her brother Thomas and her mother survived. In symbolic terms her world was being blown apart, with her restricted family unit surviving the impact together. She had this recurring dream after her father remarried:

> I dreamt of killing my dad and his wife and just laughing. But also, I used to see my mum dying in my sleep and I would not go to school next day because I was scared.

Repeatedly she now dreams of:

> Being chased through a maze by someone with no face but the maze is made of people who were laughing. I tried to scream but I could not make a noise.

Belinda has acute bouts of nervousness and shyness. No one except her asthmatic mother and best friend know of her dreams, and even they do not know that she thinks her father and his new wife have made a 'mockery' of her family's former unity. This mockery is echoed in Belinda's dreams.

Alex, now 16, recalled his earlier years:

> My mum and dad split up when I was 9, but my mum remarried when I was 11. About that time and for a few years after I had the same dream about when my mum and dad were arguing many times. My mum would scream at my dad and my dad would begin to hit her, as I stood on the stairs. I now almost hate my dad and I call my step-dad 'Dad'.

His early experiences broke the loving bond with his father and a new filial allegiance was made with his new 'dad'.

Tragic separation has been repeated many times in Leigh's short life. Now 12 years old, she continues to have a disturbing cluster of dreams:

I dream of people murdering me or my family. When I'm ill I dream that the doctors give me the wrong medicine and I die. In another one I was in a big factory and it was very scary. I was even crying in my sleep and I can feel this man stabbing me when I am sleeping. And I wake up crying. I go into the bathroom and wash my face and I think the dream will go away but it doesn't.

Her nights are filled with hideous, terror-inducing dreams. When I spoke to her she confided that two of her younger brothers died in infancy and her mother and father have split up. She said, 'I don't see that that (the deaths) has anything to do with the dreams. It's just my mum, she's forbidden me to talk about it at home or anywhere. Sometimes I feel I'll burst. I just don't know what to do.'

It is imperative that we accept that children who are part of a divorcing family feel a deep sense of loss. They often feel a profound sense of emptiness, tearfulness, an inability to concentrate, fatigue and have troublesome dreams; all are symptoms of mourning. As J. W. Worden points out, although no one has died, they mourn the death of the family of their childhood.

As we have already seen in Chapter 5, small children suffer desperately from being separated from their mothers when either has to be admitted to hospital. It was the pioneering work of John Bowlby that achieved parents' rights of unlimited hospital access to see their children. Small children in particular need someone reliable to whom they can turn when distressed or threatened. Only when such a person is available can a child develop a sense of inner security. If this security base disappears, as in separation, then the child becomes more vulnerable.

Loss

There are many areas of loss that children have to face. Loss may be of a country as well as of a person. Bashar (11), an Iraqi boy living in England temporarily, said that, 'I dream I go back to my country and me and my friends, we do a party.' However, in the spring of 1988, he had disturbing dreams about his return to his homeland, for, 'Sometimes, I dream I am going back to Iraq on an aeroplane and some men take the plane and kill me, like the Kuwaitis.'

This dream combined wish-fulfilling elements of going home, with fear triggered by the drawn-out hostage taking and hijacking of an aeroplane which had been headline news for weeks. Bashar strongly identified with those held for ransom. Tied in with his loss of roots was his fear of what might happen if he were to return to the war zone. It is an emotion shared by many young people as we shall see in the next chapter.

Moving house

Helen (13) recently moved from Suffolk to Durham, but before she did so she had several dreams about what it would be like. She said, 'In my dreams I invented people, but all my old friends were there as well.' She still dreams about her old and new friends mixed together, even though it is seven months since she relocated. Adjusting to a new place takes time and a different accent may make it even harder for some children to be accepted in the new school community.

Kirsten (17) recalled dreams from age 7 when she moved from the town to a small country village. Volcanoes and overwhelming tidal waves were the main themes but there was also a dream series. The central feature of the series was a barn in the middle of the countryside and whenever she was being chased by 'the baddies', Kirsten would always seek refuge in this barn. Gradually, through each dream, she realized that the secret hiding place she had discovered there was becoming more and more difficult to enter. Kirsten remembered that the last time she had the dream, when she was 16, she was running from enemies and gasped with relief when she saw the old familiar, fairly safe barn. She ran in the door only to be confronted with a modern milking shed made of concrete with no roof-top hiding place anymore. It was a turning point, for in the dream, she said to herself, 'Well, there's nowhere to hide now, I'm on my own.' Kirsten recognized that the dream series had been charting her growth of independence. It began when she had to actively seek new friends in a strange environment and at a new school. She was very upset about the move away from friends and a town she knew, yet was completely unable to do anything about it. Finally, when she accepted responsibility for facing up to her own problems, the barn dream disappeared – its ten-year spell was over.

Changing school

Dreams are likely to become more disturbing at times when a child leaves one school to move on to the next stage in his education. All change is stressful and children suffer stress, develop fears and have anxious thoughts about the new situation which awaits them. Listening to worries, providing information and familiarization with the new school, all help alleviate their fears. Pay attention to dream narratives for they will tell you a lot about how your child is settling down. If he is not adjusting successfully then disturbing dreams and sleep problems may become exacerbated.

Anticipation of loss

Some dreams and nightmares are a form of preparation. Frank (13), from Widnes, had a dream in which his grandmother, who is ill, died. He told me that the dream nearly made him cry but he managed to stop himself. Keeping hold of the 'strong-men-don't-cry' message, did not prevent him from realizing just how much his grandmother means to him. Her waking illness spurred him into facing the possibility of her death in his dreams.

For Tricia (14) it is a different loss that she is grappling with. She dreams that her father is critically ill in hospital or that he is leaving her because he does not want her anymore. She is struggling with becoming a separate person, independent from

Gretta (10) 'Some of my dreams are so scary that I scream. I dream I go away and I am dead.'

her father. This is hard to accept so she unconsciously projects the desire to leave on to him; he wants to leave her, he is dying, when in fact, her child stage is ending as the mature adult begins to stretch her wings.

Stan (10), described as a boy of superior intelligence, lives in America. He dreams of his chronically ill mother and of being killed by a bear. Frequently his dreams have a sad, gloomy tone, which he thinks is because he worries about his mother. He is in a permanent state of expectation that she will get worse and he will lose her.

Loss of 'self'

Children who are abused have dreams and nightmares which reflect the sense of threat, fear, isolation and invasion that they are subject to in waking life. Very little research on dreams has been done in this area, but as you have seen in earlier sections of the book, dreams do tell us of traumas that children suffer.

Patricia Garfield, in one of the rare studies on the dreams of sexually abused girls, found that their dream life differs in many ways from those of non-abused children. Chase dreams figured in over 50 per cent of their dreams but, most significantly, the chase ended in an attack on the dreamer. Not only was there attack but it usually resulted in the death of the dreamer, the mother or a younger sibling. This is not surprising since the dreamer had been subject to actual attacks when awake. Dream death, then, is a common outcome.

Children who are sexually abused are frequently told by the abuser that they will be killed if they tell anyone of the abuse. Sometimes they are told that by complying they are 'saving' a younger sibling from a similar attack. All too often the abused child feels as if part of themselves has been murdered; their right to make choices about their own body has been taken away and their trust has been killed. Dreams tell us of these feelings.

When Bernadette was 10 she used to dream of being attacked by a bull. Though her sister was there, she did nothing to save Bernadette. She also dreamt of being held prisoner in an underground cell. She described her childhood: 'My home was broken. My sisters and I were battered, there were constant rows, very little money. We had to stay upstairs out of the way. At the time I did not think I was unhappy.' Now she realizes just how damaging her experiences were. Her early abusive experiences scarred her emotionally and intimate, trusting relationships, now she is an adult, are immensely difficult. For children who receive supportive therapy this need not be the outcome.

While many children have anxiety dreams about being pursued by an anonymous stranger, abused children are much more likely to dream of the actual molester. The chief emotion in the dreams is helplessness. This was obvious in a dream recounted to me by a 16-year-old girl. She had a recurring dream of being stripped naked, tied to a plank and being beaten and raped. At the end of the dream she is in a block of ice which preserves her. Gina was actually raped at the age of 12 and the nightmare had recurred regularly since then. Her attackers replay their role in her dreams. The theme of helplessness, of being tied down, paralysed and powerless, is beyond doubt. Also, the need to freeze in the face of sexual or physical attack, which is a common response for children in this appalling situation, is symbolically represented in the 'block of ice' in Gina's dream.

Patricia Garfield noticed in her research that difficulties in breathing, or choking, were also common themes of sexually abused youngsters and quotes a dream in which the dreamer was drowning in a white glue, symbolizing semen. The woman had been raped in childhood and was forced into oral sex.

Nightmares and sleep disturbances are highly significant indicators of child sexual abuse. Some experts say that in older children, the first sign of sexual abuse may be sexually explicit acting-out behaviour, while nightmares come next. Certainly in any case of child abuse nightmares and sleep disturbances increase. Barbara Myers, a former victim, describes the indefensible in an open letter to her father:

You destroyed my ability to sleep, to think, to develop. My nights were horrors. I used to lie awake in bed and worry whether you were going to come into my room. Sometimes the night fears would overtake me and I would dream – or perhaps hallucinate – evil things happening. Sometimes you would take me from my room and tell me I had sleep-walked. You destroyed my trust in my own sanity.

Child-abuse statistics make grim reading. Current research by E. Bass and L. Thornton indicates that one in four girls and one in seven boys will be sexually abused by the age of twelve. This means that most of us will come in contact with someone – family, friend, neighbour, colleague – who has suffered abuse. If you are concerned with the welfare of children, listen to their dreams when they share them and be alert to signals they send. As Lord Justice Butler-Sloss said in her report on the Cleveland inquiry, there are not enough people listening to what children say.

Death

Many people are surprised to learn that children think and dream about death quite frequently. Often such dreams are prompted by waking events such as the death of a pet, a television programme or a book. Other triggers, though, are the need we have to comprehend mortality and the place of death in our society. Also, in dreams, death very often symbolizes the ending of one phase of life and the beginning of another.

Gretta (10) found a ladybird. Wanting to keep it as a pet, she put it in a matchbox, as many children do, but it died. When her sister also died suddenly, Gretta became troubled by disturbing dreams. She dreamt that huge, slug-like creatures were climbing up the outside wall of her house and into her bedroom. She had recurring dreams of rows upon rows of grey crosses in an endless cemetery. Nothing happened other than the defeating repetition of gravestones continuing into infinity.

These dreams include a number of common features found in dreams connected with death. At a simple level there is Gretta's guilt at killing the harmless ladybird which she wanted to keep. Her dream invaders are similarly of the insect world and are out to wreak revenge, as it appears to a sensitive 10-year-old. Then there is the enormity of her sister's death; Gretta suddenly learns that death goes on and on, thousands upon thousands of dream headstones reiterate the truth she has had to face. The dream enables her to contemplate a powerful truth. It is a way for her psyche to give her space to consider and reflect. In the normal, externally organized, busy, fast pace of many children's lives, there is little time to sit and think without interruptions from family and friends against a background of television or radio. Her dreams are part of the processing of her trauma.

Gretta's slug dream also mirrors her waking thoughts about being eaten by worms and fearful fantasies she had had about her sister's burial and its consequences. Her dreams allowed expression of thoughts. If a child asks, 'Will worms eat her?', she is usually shushed and told not to talk like that. The thoughts do not go away but have to be dealt with in some way; the dreaming process allows this to take place.

Stefan (14) dreams of becoming a hero by saving someone's life. However, judging by his other dreams, I think it may be his own life he is trying to save:

> My dream is always about someone going after my friends with a gun and I kill the man. It is my dad that I kill ... Sometimes I dream about my gran coming to kill me and then she puts me in the grave. She died a year ago. I have always been having dreams about people going to die.

He could recall no happy dreams other than a dream in which he flew off to space. In another dream he was drowning. He asked me to tell children not to worry about bad dreams because he knows his grandmother loved him and would not want to to harm him. But there is so much unresolved pain and grief for Stefan. In the space on the questionnaire which says, 'Please tell me about yourself and your life,' he wrote: 'I live with my mum and my two sisters. My dad left when I was 5.' Then there was something heavily crossed out, but followed by the words, 'I hate him for that.' Stefan's calm exterior belies the anger he feels about being left by his father and then his grandmother.

Images of death

Melody (10) mostly dreams about people being killed. One nightmare she describes:

> My childminder left me and some friends on the Yorkshire Moors. We wandered around for a day, then we saw a field of 'unicorn sheep'. We wanted to go in it so I went in and all the sheep stood still. When I got to a lamb it charged me. My friend went in and got charged and killed. Then we got taken to another friend's house where we ate my friend. I remember the taste. Dad said, 'Who wants the brain? Very good for you.' The brain was like a white bar of soap. Ugh!!

Melody has another dream in which she goes to school only to find that the bins, basins and drawers contain dead people preserved in stale, soapy water. She says that in the dream:

> My friends didn't mind and casually talked about it. At swimming they walked back and on the trees hung dead bodies. My friends said things like, 'I used to know him from play school . . .'

Melody seemed very composed about these dreams. She wants to write crime books when she is older – I wonder whether this reflects a particular turn of mind necessary for a crime writer? Certainly she displays no squeamishness. She reads avidly and loves books like *The Lord of the Rings*. She hates to be copied and strives to be a strong individualist. Her dreams were the only ones of their type that I have heard from a child of this age.

Death of the dreamer

Adolescence is a time of great emotional turmoil and a number of young people told me of dreams in which they were killed by others or by their own hand. David (15), who has recurrent episodes of suicidal behaviour, recalled that in his earliest self-destructive dream: 'I was jumping off a house and floating down. Then I tried it again and still I floated down.' This he repeated until the dream ended.

Suicide attempts, successful and unsuccessful, are not rare among adolescents. Since 1975 suicide has been identified as the third leading cause of death among adolescents in the USA. Having to relinquish ties of dependency to parents and form close-bonds with others causes stress and upheaval. For some young people, maybe because of mental health problems in the family, poor economic conditions, disturbed family dynamics and feelings of powerlessness, the task of living appears too difficult.

There is a strong link between severely stressful life events and suicide attempts. Critical life events, such as a death in the family, separation, illness and so on, cause major upheavals in

Kerry (9) 'I dreamed that Daddy was killing Mummy.'

our psyches. Being too vulnerable under stress may then lead to suicidal behaviour.

All the time, when we are considering young people, we must bear in mind that what the adolescent sees as stressful may not be the same as the adult. We must really listen to the feelings young people tell us they have, not assume that we know; nor must we listen only to that which fits with our preconceptions. On a simple level, if we know that a young person is experiencing increased stress there is an increased risk of self-destructive behaviour. Dreams may be one way of ascertaining just how vulnerable that person is and so they may give an early warning signal.

When Wendy (14) was 10 she dreamt that she was dead and saw the flowers at her funeral. Kate (15), from Londonderry, described a similar dream in more detail:

> I was dead. I seen people sitting around me crying, then I seen my funeral. It was raining and everyone in my family was crying bitterly.

A Hardy-like setting with mourning relatives keening their loss, reflects Kate's depressed moods when she feels 'they' will only really appreciate her when she has gone. A similar mood emanates from Janette's dream.

Belfast-born Janette (13) describes her own funeral in great detail:

> When I had the measles I dreamt that I died and I came to my funeral. I saw myself laying in the coffin. It was blue marble and I was laying on a light blue silk sheet and I had my hands crossed on my chest. And while I was in the coffin dead, I was also at my own funeral, crying and laying flowers down by the coffin. Then I woke up and looked at myself in the mirror to make sure I was there.

Barnaby (14), a patient in an adolescent psychiatric unit, dreams of dying and wonders how painful it is. He has been in care now for six months, after life with his mother and stepfather became intolerable. His happiest dream is one in which he is no longer in care, but is living with his natural father in Canada – a place he has never been to with a man he has seen only twice. His waking fantasies show up as wish-fulfilment dreams and serve as some escape from his unhappy waking life.

Madeline (15), who has lived in a children's home since her parents' separation and the breakdown in her ability to control her own behaviour, finds that for the first time in years she has begun to trust those around her. It is a tremendously underrated task, learning to trust again, or maybe for the first time, and while it has enormous rewards, it is a painful learning process:

> The most frightening dream I had was that one of the staff from the children's home had died, and I would not accept it, because Trevor (the staff) has helped me a lot.

He has helped her understand the causes of her own erratic mood swings and disturbing behaviour. So many conflicts are now appreciated because they are in context, not isolated pieces of a jigsaw that show no picture. Consequently, Madeline is beginning to have more self-confidence and self-respect. Though her future remains unsure she has a deeper sense of self, which is a healthier starting point from which to go forward.

Sudden death

Grieving is a necessary part of responding to death in a healthy way. It is normal to have a wide range of responses to death; to feel sorrow, to feel anger, perhaps at being left behind to cope with ongoing problems, to feel guilt, perhaps because we feel we should have done more but were too busy. These reactions are to be expected. Where death has been unexpected or in unusual circumstances, however, grieving can be a much more problematic experience. Where this happens as a result of a war or civil disturbance there are additional factors to consider. Dreams related to war are dealt with in depth in the next chapter.

Felice Cohen records her work with a little boy, Mark, whose brother had died in a fire inadvertently started by both boys. Mark was referred to her for therapy two years after the fire. At that time he had a range of problematic symptoms; he ate compulsively, hit and bit himself, disobeyed his parents and provoked fights with family and friends. He seemed constantly to seek out punishment. The situation was becoming intolerable.

Mark's parents did not openly express their grief, and their son was ignored, left unconsoled and not given any opportunity to vent his grief. Understandably they found their own ambivalent feelings towards their remaining son extremely difficult to cope with. Felice says that after four months of painting pictures he began to accompany his drawings with descriptions of his tormented dreams in which red hot fires consumed him. He asked why he had not been allowed to go to the funeral, why his parents would not talk to him about Scotty and asked why he, too, could not have died. That was the turning point in his therapy. No one had ever explained what had happened, no one had ever used the word accident in reference to the tragedy, and stuck in his mind was the image that Scotty was taken away and no one ever mentioned him again. After a further three months in art therapy, working through his grief and realizing that he had not murdered his brother, Mark's original problems were eliminated. He and his parents were able to be more open emotionally and they were able to share as a family once more.

David (16) told me that he mainly dreams about death. For instance, his most frightening dream was:

> When I was involved in a car crash and all my family died, only I lived and I was paralysed and unable to kill myself.

I wondered why this theme was so prevalent. Then he described his happiest dream:

> I went back into the past and changed everything that happened on the fifth of May, because that was the day my younger brother was killed in a cycling accident.

David had to face the tragic reality of sudden death and he could not be protected from its harshness. Regrettably some children are actually misled about death rather than protected. In an attempt to soften the blow we may be tempted to say, 'Mummy has gone away,' and the child waits and waits for her return; or, 'Grandad was very tired. He feel asleep and he didn't wake up.' This may lead to great confusion and fear and the bereaved child may be afraid to sleep in case the same thing happens to him. Children, anyway, confuse sleep with death, and such explanations serve to increase the confusion.

Bringing them back in dreams

Children come to terms with death in all sorts of ways. Some believe that after death they will come alive again. Partly this is to do with watching television programmes where the almost-dead rise in time for the next episode, and partly to do with religious beliefs about life after death. The need to believe in our own immortality is a very primitive, forceful power.

Death of a significant person in life is a devastating experience for children. One of the ways we make up for the physical loss may be by imagining the person who has died and, as an extension of this, dreaming that the loved one is with us once more. Stuart (12) does this:

> I dream that my grandad, who's dead, sits at the end of my bed and sings to me.

Some children would envy Stuart's dream in that they too wish for such a comforting dream which serves as a reminder of good times gone by. But they sleep in vain and their wishes are not fulfilled; such dreams do not come. Yet others wish that they could forget a death, as did Cassie (14), from Canada, whose mother died when she was 7. Repeated dreams of her death haunt Cassie, leaving her sad and debilitated.

Other young people have more helpful dreams about dead relatives. For instance, Deborah, though very upset when her grandfather died, found some solace in a dream where he told her that he was happy and well and that Deborah and the rest of the family need not be upset. The dream released, it gave her permission to finish grieving and move forward in her life.

During their development children naturally experience a stage where they have fears, often at bedtime, that their parents will die. Such fears and dreams can be terrifying. It is very distressing for adults too. To sit and comfort a child who says, 'Mummy, you're not going to die are you? You won't die will you?' is painful because it forces you to face the fact that you may in fact die before this dependent child grows up. There are no guarantees for any of us. We have to find ways of reassuring our children and empowering them emotionally so that they can cope with loss.

Children fear their own death, which is again very distressing for parent and child alike. These are crucial concepts that we grapple with and they are not comfortable. There are no pat phrases to explain feelings that touch the very depth of our being.

Justine (15) told me of her dream:

In reality my father died nearly six years ago of leukaemia. I dreamt not long ago that the doorbell went and he was standing on the doorstep with all his cases ready to come home.

It needs no interpretation to explain Justine's wish-fulfilment dream.

Martyn (12) told me that his father died when he was 6

months old and his grandmother died when he was 10 years old. He himself has been in and out of hospital and so it is not surprising that his dreams should be concerned with these themes. His most frightening dream:

My dad, my aunt and my nana – who are all dead now – were sitting on the settee and they were saying witchcraft and when I woke up I could hear the witchcraft all day.

In this dream he shows a conspiracy against him, which is how much of his waking life feels.

Maxwell (9) told me about his dream:

In my dream all the family was at the crematorium. My grandad had died. The coffin was just about to disappear behind the curtains. The vicar was just saying, 'Now Sidney G— is to be cremated.' Just then there came a croaking noise from the coffin. It started to open and Grandad got out of it. And after that everything was alright.

Maxwell's mother added, 'On the third night after Grandad died, my husband too had a similar dream to Maxwell's. He dreamt that there was knock on the door and the doctor appeared with my husband's dad. He said they'd taken Grandad to hospital and that they'd removed something from his throat and that he was perfectly alright. Both my husband and Maxwell rarely remember their dreams but this dream woke them and they were able to recall it. The next day we talked about the dreams and Grandad's death at length. Maxwell said that he knew Grandad was now happy in heaven with Granny, he just wished he was still with us.'

Maxwell is fortunate to have a mother who is willing to talk about one of the remaining taboo areas in our society. It is a taboo that has been around for a long time. Charles Darwin, great scientific explorer and pioneer of his generation, suffered throughout his life from chronic ill health. Evidence tells us it was psychiatric and psychosomatic in origin. His mother died when he was only 9 years of age and two of his three sisters would not allow the mother's name ever to be mentioned.

Ruby (6) 'There was a woman being killed with a knife. The man tried to kill me too but I ran away.'

Darwin himself, in later years, said he could remember nothing about her at all. The overwhelming taboo drove his pain into the darkness of the unconscious and its only expression was through continued illness.

What can we tell the children?

As we have seen, children dream about death and they think about it. Telling them not to worry about it does not help. From an early age children need honesty and simple, straightforward explanations.

Very young children taste grief. Bowlby concluded, in his work on attachment and loss in children's lives, that children as young as fifteen months experienced loss in the same way as adults. They go through the four common stages of mourning: an initial numbness with occasional bouts of intense anger or distress, then searching and yearning for the lost person, disorganization and despair, and finally, if all goes well, there is a reconciliation and acceptance of the loss. This grieving process of denial, anger, guilt and acceptance, may last for many months; two years is a common period needed. It is a fallacy that children rapidly forget about death, they do not. So allow time and be patient.

A significant difference between adult mourning and that of children, is that children are less in control of their lives. They may be sent to school when in fact they want time alone or in the company of a loved parent, or they may want to go and play with friends but feel they will be told off if they express that desire. Help them to understand that such wide-ranging moods are natural and avoid inadvertently inducing guilt by being shocked if they want to have fun.

Listen to children and their needs – do not assume you know what they want; give them space to think and talk. Help them to cope with conflicting messages at school where they may be encouraged by some to talk of their bereavement but have it ignored by others who insist on the insensitive 'pull-yourself together' or 'it's-nothing-to-do-with-me' approach. At all events there may be intense pressure to keep strong emotions under control. Rosemary Wells, who was widowed when her children were 11, 14 and 17, wrote *Helping Children Cope with Grief*. It extends the number of strategies available to anyone involved with children experiencing bereavement.

If the death has been of a parent, there is the added burden that the remaining parent may be so upset herself that she cannot cope with the child's grief as well. Just when the child needs most stability and parental love he may be sent away to relatives and has additional separation to deal with, without the security of his usual environment.

There may be a powerful message that the display of grief on the child's part is making things worse so it should be suppressed. So run the general admonitions to 'be strong' and not cry. This may cause long-term psychological damage. Children must be allowed to work through their own pain and loss without being made to feel guilty about it. To grieve as a family is a powerfully healing experience.

There is no right way to tell children about death. Be as honest as you can, avoid misunderstandings and answer their questions in as open a way as possible. Sensitive support and reassurance that they will still be cared for and loved by those who remain, enable a child to grieve and to rebuild feelings of security.

NINE

Children Dream of War

What causes dreams of war?

Dreams about war come from many sources; from stories children hear from grandparents, from films, from history lessons at school, from the news they watch on television. They learn of war and experience fear. Those who live in war zones actually live the terror their dreams portray.

The dreams of young people reflect what they may only be aware of on a subliminal level. For instance, when Myrtle was 11 and World War II had just broken out, her parents were thinking of sending her to Canada, out of harm's way.

I told my mother about this dream where I was with crowds of people. There was a ship and all over the sea was white wool. It was an awful dream and I woke up very frightened.

Unknown to Myrtle her mother had begun knitting in white wool. She was making jackets for children being evacuated to Canada and was considering whether or not she should send her daughter away . . .

Myrtle did not go to Canada but about the time she was due to go, a ship was bombed and all the children were lost. An early indication of psychic ability that became more pronounced as Myrtle reached adulthood? Or was this dream an expression of her fears at being evacuated? Now 60 years old, Myrtle has discovered that her psychic ability has been passed on to her daughter, who also has warning dreams.

Waking experience of German raids, which left the sky alight with flames, and her taste of fear as she was evacuated from the

Channel Islands in the hold of a ship, affected May's dreams for many years. Until she was in her 20s she repeatedly dreamt that a patch of forget-me-nots was being crushed by a large boot. There was an indescribable smell attached to the dream too, which May found very upsetting. Looking back she realized that to cope with the stress, she put herself in a kind of limbo, shutting out feelings and keeping herself closed off from the dangerous world of the 1940s.

People I have spoken to who were children during the last world war recalled dreams of being bombed or of being separated from family. Separation, as we saw in the last chapter, is particularly hard to bear. Separation also brought new responsibilities to Julia, the eldest in her family:

> One night, in my tenth year, the six of us, including my mother were there. That evening Dad was telling us that he was going off to the war. He was in the habit of cleaning all the shoes. Pointing to me and my younger sister he said that Mother would have such a lot to do that we would have to help by cleaning the shoes. I dreamt that night that the Germans had come. They locked me in a room like a library but instead of books on the shelves there were rows and rows of really dirty shoes. I was told that I had to stay there without anything to eat or drink until I had cleaned them all.

In a panic Julia woke up. Her new responsibilities were obviously taken very seriously; in her dream her very survival was dependent on carrying them out.

Such dreams often recur at times when the dreamer is stressed. The increased anxiety of a present situation evokes memories of past anxieties and triggers the dreams. Later in this chapter we will look at strategies which are helpful in coping with such dreams.

Ruth (10) dreamt that Russia and America had a fight and they blew up the whole world. She drew a child calling, 'Help' and a sad-faced woman shouting 'Where are my children?'. Another figure with tears flowing to the floor says, 'We are all going to die.' Ruth said everyone would be killed and no one would be alive after this war.

Ruth has no direct, personal experience of war, though she is affected by it. Personal experience of war makes a profound impact. In a recent study, commissioned by Prince Talal bin Abdul-Aziz, it was found that more than 58 per cent of Lebanese children are suffering from stress-related illnesses because of the civil war there. Children nearer home suffer similar stress and we will consider the dreams of children in conflict-scarred Northern Ireland in more detail later in the chapter, but first, here is an account of a girl who knew war first hand.

Allsama (13) has been in England for just six months. Her family came from Iraq so that her father could get treatment after being wounded in the Iran–Iraq war. Allsama wants to be a soldier when she grows up. Still very bitter about her father's injuries, she would like the opportunity to avenge him and kill her 'Iranian and Jewish enemies'. Her dreams reflect her wartime experiences. She dreams of being in the army; of Jewish soldiers hitting Palestinians and fighting against the Iranians with guns. Indeed, her happiest dream is that, 'The Jewish people have left the West Bank.' She has lived her whole life, to date, soaking up the sectarian view of the world in which she lives, just as children in the opposing camp have soaked up the views and norms of their side. Children learn to hate during war. Tribal loyalties become further entrenched.

The continuing horror of conflict in Northern Ireland affects children in England too. James (9), who lives in Manchester, dreamt that, 'All the Irish people were bombing the English people and people kept getting killed.' Although not directly exposed to the violence, he sees reports on television and in newspapers and hears people talking about the situation. His suppressed waking anxiety is aired in his dreams.

Other dreams of war may be unexpectedly triggered. For example, Gary (12), from Widnes, explained that a nearby chemical firm uses an air-raid siren when work shifts change. 'That', he says, 'sometimes starts me off thinking about war and then it starts war dreams.' Paul (9), on the other hand, is an avid comic reader and dreams about bazookas, bomb-dropping aircraft and nuclear submarines. Unconsciously he projects his internally felt anger on to external objects, as many of us do. It is much more comfortable to put the anger out there rather than accept the 'badness' within.

An interest in warfare and militaria influenced Ian's dreams. A keen model-kit maker, Ian (14) found that distressing nightmares were an unexpected side effect of his enthusiasm:

> I can recall being trapped in the cockpit of a fighter plane during a dogfight in World War II, over the sea. The cockpit jammed and the plane was on fire. Just as I was about to crash into the sea I woke up panting and sweating.

War stories we tell the children

In America 15 per cent of returned Vietnam war veterans are suffering from post-traumatic stress disorder, a condition we examined in Chapter 5. Indeed, such was the affect of the Vietnam war and aftermath on American soldiers that more have died by their own hand since their return than died in the war. Characteristically, sleep disorders and recurrent dreams of death and dismemberment cause them intense distress. Their dreams stem from actually fighting in a war. Some soldiers tell children stories of the war, which in turn infect the children's dreams.

Many who lived through a war tell the heroic side of the story to eager young listeners. They often omit the worst parts so that children may develop a warped view of what war is really all about. This view is compounded by the glamorization often found in Rambo-style films. Andrew (11) spoke of one of his dreams:

> We were all at war down our road. Germans at one side and the English at the other. We all had guns. We stood at the top of the house shooting out of the windows. Everyone was shot except me. It was up to me to kill all the Germans that were left.
>
> I had one gun and a bit of ammo left. Hitler was going in every house with his men checking if anyone was hiding. I

had to hide quickly. I locked the door and ran to the old cupboard in the corner of the room ... I could hear him coming. I heard the sound of gunfire. I thought he must be opening the locked door ...

One man came into the room I was in. I jumped out and shot him. The others must have heard, they all came running in. I shot the next man ... I knew that I could kill them all. Two men came in then I shot one of them but the other one killed me. Then suddenly I woke up.

The heroic boy saves the day.

Other boys dream of fighting and killing Hitler, but Nancy (12), from Cheshire, is unusual in that she dreamt that she went back in time to World War I but she was a man fighting and had lots of medals.

If your child tells you about a 'war' dream, note the details of the dream. Does it have echoes of your everyday life, as 8-year-old Rupert's did?

My mum and dad were in a war. The Germans kept dropping bombs on our farm, killing the cattle and wounding the family. The dogs and cats escaped with me through a secret passage near our oil tank.

Rupert has his remote Yorkshire farm as the setting of the dream with his parents and farm animals around him. His parents are 'in a war', which might damage him and his pets but he finds a hidden escape route. Often such details are important. Here, Rupert gives voice to his anxieties about his parents' relationship, about their 'war'.

Racism

In her diary Anne Frank wrote of her nocturnal dreams and her intense desire for peace. Subject to the inhuman policies the Nazis implemented in Germany, she eventually died in a concentration camp. Fifteen thousand children were deported to Terezin concentration camp near Prague, surely one of the most harrowing examples of the ultimate injustices of racism. One little girl who survived wrote a poem quoted in Kübler-Ross, *On Children and Death*:

> *I'd Like To Go Alone*
>
> I'd like to go away alone,
> Where there are other, nicer people
> Somewhere into the far unknown,
> There, where no one kills another.

A number of children recalled dreams of the Holocaust, Jews and non-Jews alike. Paul (11) explained:

> The most frightening dream I had was fighting a war with Germany and I was put in a chamber of gas.

Hannah (12), a member of a flourishing Jewish youth group, said that her most frightening dream was when she was caught up in the Holocaust and was in a concentration camp. After studying *The Diary of Anne Frank* in literature classes other children found their dreams peopled with her characters.

The young poet quoted above may have recalled a dream like Imran's. Imran (16), living in the North-West, described a dream which I found in slightly different forms among the majority of children of Asian origin. You can see the undisguised desire for peace and tranquillity here too:

> The happiest dream I ever had was about being on an island all by myself with only my thoughts for company. It was always peaceful. No trouble.

He had been the subject of much racial abuse at school and was frightened to go out alone. Sometimes his home comes under attack and being ever-vigilant has become a way of life.

Many children in this country suffer racial abuse and it showed markedly in the dreams of those of Asian origin. For example, Najwa (10), born in England of Pakistani parents, has suffered many verbal assaults and numerous threatened physical attacks:

My most frightening dream was, I was riding on my bike and my daddy was sweeping the garden and this man was being nasty to this boy so my daddy started to tell him off, but he just kicked him and then he came and took me away.

Shaista (11), whose mother is a teacher and whose father is a factory owner, when asked if she talked to anyone about her dreams, replied: 'I don't talk to anyone unless they know me very well, so that they don't start picking on me.' She decided that she would tell me:

I had to light fire to my house when everybody was asleep because two people came in and thought my dad was a bank manager and they wanted to rob the bank without my dad finding out, so they told me to light fire to my house, but I didn't and they lit fire to me.

Her nightmare, told to me after a number of fire attacks on the homes of Asians had been reported in the Press, reveals her unvocalized fears.

The threat of nuclear war

'A weapon is an enemy even to its owner' – Turkish proverb.

According to the Medical Campaign Against Nuclear Weapons, the world now spends £2,500 a second on nuclear arms. The testing of the weapons seriously damages health, and fear of the consequences affects our children. Studies from countries all round the world show that the fear is greatest in the early teens and then diminishes as more effective coping mechanisms are developed, or as ego defences grow stronger. All studies reviewed at the 1988 conference of the Medical Campaign Against Nuclear Weapons showed nuclear war was the third or fourth fear of young people after parental death, exam failure and, in Britain, unemployment. A typical example of the way in which dreams reflect the nuclear fear is given by Elizabeth (14). She has had this recurring nightmare for the past two years:

I was in my bedroom, which is very small, and so were all my

Ruth (10) '*In my dream America and Russia had a fight and the world is blowing up.*'

friends, relatives and family friends. It was as if everyone I knew and cared for was there in my small room and we were all together and safe. The sky outside was an orange colour and it was hot in the room. Somehow we knew there was a fire. We didn't know where; it was everywhere. It was very humid and the sky got redder and redder and it got hotter and hotter. A war siren was going off and we knew it was a nuclear war and that the world was hot and it was as if it was on fire.

Dr Eric Chivian, staff psychiatrist at the Massachusetts Institute of Technology, writing in *The Human Cost of Nuclear War*, commented that children have been robbed of a belief in the future, fearful as they are that their future will be annihilated by nuclear weapons. He found in his study of American children's knowledge of and response to nuclear issues that children absorbed messages of anxiety and despair from their culture. One 7-year-old girl said that she sometimes thought she would rather be dead because then she could go to heaven and would not have to worry about 'all this stuff about nuclear war'.

Nightmares about nuclear devastation are widespread. Marc (15) has a recurring dream which includes typical elements: fear, being alone, feeling powerless and a sense of irreversible, impending doom:

I am quite a way from my house and it is a really hot sunny day. High up in the sky I see a nuclear missile moving slowly across the sky. It is coming in my neighbourhood's direction. I start to run towards my house but I always lapse into slow motion and the missile is catching me up. I have never made it to my house and I always wake up as the bomb goes off.

Lee Anne (14) dreamt she was blinded in a nuclear explosion and she had to survive with the effects of a bomb which had dropped near her street. Joanne (16) had a dream of nuclear war after watching *Threads*; in her dream she was one of the people depicted in the film. First-hand accounts of nuclear explosions are equally disturbing.

After the bombing of Nagasaki, Dr Akizuki's consulting room was swamped with burnt victims. He reveals the reality survivors faced and his own childhood dream:

Half naked or stark naked, they walked with strange, slow steps, groaning from deep inside themselves, as if they had travelled from the depths of hell. They looked whitish; their faces were like masks. I felt as if I were dreaming, watching pallid ghosts processing slowly in one direction – as in a dream I had once dreamt in my childhood.

The reality and the dream have much in common, as do the dreams being dreamed by children today.

Abandoned

Many children feel abandoned by adults and the society in which they live. In a recent British *Guardian* survey among 10- to 17-year olds, worries about nuclear weapons and war figured prominently as these dreams reveal. A recurring dream image is of being totally alone or in the company of strangers either just before a nuclear attack or in the wake of one. In vain the dreamers search for family and friends.

Richard (16) had a series of nuclear-war dreams when he was 12. He said, 'When the bomb dropped I always seemed to be alone, not with anyone I knew, and I think that is what frightened me.' The message seems to be that there is no one to protect him from this horror, he is alone. Another 16-year-old, Melany, commented:

> I dreamt that nuclear war broke out. It was frightening because of the few minutes leading up to it, everyone rushed about not knowing what to do. I was left alone but these faces which were distorted kept appearing wherever I turned.

Margaret (11) attends a primary school in England:

> Once I dreamt that nuclear war broke out and Ireland was blown up and my family and I were all on different parts of the world and I was just floating on a very, very small plot of land. The rest of the world had sunk under the sea . . .

She was able to wake to her mother's reassuring voice. But how easy is it to be comforting, especially if you live in the shadow of a nuclear power station and your child attends a school in which a store of anti-radiation pills are kept 'just in case' there is an accident?

The end of the world

Time and again young people who took part in this research spoke of their most frightening dream being one in which there was a nuclear war that destroyed the whole world. There is a terror that the dreams will become a reality. Young children like Samantha (11) were so upset by the annihilation of family and the world they knew, that they too wanted to die rather than live on alone. Helena (15) had a dream which epitomizes this fear:

> It was about a nuclear war. A lot of drummers came into my room and dragged me outside. My brother and mum were there. They were putting barbed wire along the bushes. They were in camouflage and had black on their faces. I too was like that. We were in the garage. It had been decorated and had pretty curtains. I took some sleeping tablets, kissed my mum and brother goodnight. I started crying. When I woke up I did actually have tears in my eyes and I couldn't stop myself from crying.

Panic is another aspect of nuclear-war dreams, as Faith (16) relates:

> The most frightening dream I have ever had is about the world ending. The people on my street all came running out of their houses yelling and I couldn't find my mum so I went to look for her. I wanted to save my mum. The next thing I can remember is counting down the seconds to the world blowing up.

Dreams of the end of the world often start at home, so for Shebnam (10) her school and hometown represent the world:

> I dreamt we were at my primary school and we heard that World War III was going to start so we had to hide in our classes with the teachers and I saw this great big man saying, 'It's coming', very loudly and a big bomb came and blew up Milnrow.

For Darren (11), too, war was closely tied to home:

> I have a dream that Widnes got invaded by the Germans. They blew up Widnes with a bomb and I never saw my mum and dad again.

Ordinarily, childhood fears of spiders or monsters can be tackled in a reassuring way. We can say that spiders are small and usually harmless; we can say that those horrible monsters of TV and books are not to be found stalking the streets, but we cannot say that nuclear warheads are really safe. After Chernobyl, nobyl, we cannot say accidents with nuclear power will not happen. Parents have no platitudes to offer that can adequately comfort children. What we can do is avoid denying the anxiety that the child has, and we can also fight for a safer future – and planet – for our children. Research in America, carried out by paediatrician Tony Waterson, indicates that children of peace activists feel more confident about their future and more hopeful that we can avoid nuclear war.

Not all dreams about nuclear war end in catastrophe. Seth

(12) dreamt that although the Russians had set off a bomb, Superman caught it and threw it into space! And for some young people disbelief proves an effective barrier, as Emily (15) explained: 'I never have dreams about a nuclear war. I know some people of my age are really terrified of it but I don't seem to worry about it too much. That's probably because I can't believe there will ever be one.'

Children at war now

Since 1945 there has not been a single day on which the world has been at peace. War has raged somewhere on earth: Vietnam, Mozambique, South Africa, Lebanon, Ireland, the Falklands. What effect does this have on children now?

The thirteen-year war in Beirut is familiar to us through television news but less well known is the effect on the children who live there. Mai Masri and Jean Chamoum, Beirut residents and film makers, noted that while the children seemingly cope with the anger and strife, their only games are war games. The facts of life for children there are chilling: since 1975 14,000 children have been kidnapped and 10,000 of these have been found dead, 17,000 have disappeared, 100,000 have been orphaned and 100,000 are street fighters. Families live under conditions of acute stress. The children suffer waking and sleeping nightmares.

Northern Ireland

It was obvious when I began to examine the thousands of dreams sent to me that there were striking differences between the dreams of children in Northern Ireland and those who lived in the rest of the United Kingdom.

Children in Northern Ireland had 21 per cent more dreams of killing than children on the mainland. They had significantly more dreams of death, war, and illness. They were more likely to dream of being attacked and had more nightmares. They mentioned religious images in dreams more often too. Was this just because Northern Irish children were very different from their mainland peers I wondered? When comparing dreams which had a neutral emotional impact, for example dreams of animals or school, I discovered that the figures were proportionally almost identical to figures in the UK. The dreams of Northern Irish children reflect the way in which they are exposed to psychological and physical threat.

The effects of violence

Many children who live in this troubled part of the world have dreams which mirror the daily drama of conflict. They dream of terrorists, gunmen, funerals and war. Nichola (12), whose uncle was killed in the horrific Milltown Cemetery attack, is no stranger to street warfare and her dreams are affected:

> When we had only just moved into our house and we were unpacking, I was upstairs putting my toys away when I heard a gun shot and saw a man with a gun in our backyard, so I ran downstairs and told my mammy and daddy. They went out the back and saw nothing but later that night when my mammy was putting up the curtains she saw a man with blood all over his face at the window. He shouted, 'Nichola, Nichola!', but it was my mammy waking me up for school.

The blood-streaked man is seeking Nichola and she is afraid. At first her parents cannot see this intruder as perhaps they cannot see just how terrified she sometimes feels in waking life. She recognized that one of the reasons we dream is to relieve anxiety, for she comments, 'We need to dream to sort out a problem or because we have something on our minds which causes us to have stress and we have to think it over . . .'

Children's learning, behaviour and attitudes are affected by exposure to violence. The vocabulary of dreams tells us what children have learnt as we see in Emma's dream:

> I dreamt that two people out of my class were chasing the rest of my class with machine guns and bombs and hand grenades . . .

Finn (7) Children in Northern Ireland reported more dreams of kidnapping, being attacked or having themes of death in dreams than did children in the rest of the British Isles.

Ten-year-old Emma's father was shot one night as he was walking home in the Ardoyne district of Belfast, so it is not surprising that his daughter should dream of the hardware of war. Erin (11) is also from the Ardoyne:

> Once I dreamt about a man who was a member of the army, who got blew up right in front of my eyes. Then I got shot three times in the eyes so I couldn't identify the person who blew the soldier up.

A terrifying picture of a child innocently witnessing an act, yet in her dream she also becomes a victim. Many children's dreams express fear of paramilitary groups, from either side of the sectarian divide. Like many children living in conditions of war, Erin knows that very little special consideration will be given to her because she is a child.

Direct exposure to the violence in Northern Ireland and

repeated exposure to televised reports of violence in the province makes it seem almost normal and therefore acceptable. A large-scale research project with schoolboys, undertaken by J. L. Russell, suggests that many who usually watched Ulster violence on their screens were more likely to accept civil disorder as a way of achieving their political goals. Waking and dreaming views of the world are affected by the 'troubles'. In fact one effect may have been to push adolescents into conformity with parents rather than into customary adolescent rebellion against them. The everyday happenings in Northern Ireland may swamp the usual conflicts between generations, so generation-gap family squabbles do not figure so markedly.

Dreams are influenced in many ways. Colette (15), from Londonderry, explained:

> I dream about people and events that have happened, such as operations, bombs and close family dying as well as happy events like weddings and parties. If there has been anybody killed or shot by the IRA or if a no-warning bomb has gone off, like the one at Enniskillen, I dream about it.

These are very typical themes for youngsters in Northern Ireland in the Eighties. Colette's further comments are also revealing:

> I dreamt there was a bomb outside my house and nobody came to help my brother and me. And my brother couldn't move and neither could I. My brother died and I couldn't do anything to help him and in my dream I felt very guilty.

Powerless, unaided and the victim of seemingly arbitrary violence, Colette still takes up a burden of responsibility for her brother. Yet, because of the civil war, he has left Londonderry to live abroad. In her happiest dream she brings both her brothers who have moved away home again. The war in Northern Ireland has not only robbed her of a basic feeling of ordinary security experienced by those living on the mainland of Great Britain, it has also robbed her of family connection. Emigration from both Northern Ireland and Southern Ireland is taking on epic proportions last seen during the devastating potato famine of the 1840s.

Often dreams of bombing come after there has been a reported incident. The dreams deal with the debris of the waking experience and attempt to classify and order it. Imelda (15), from Londonderry, told me that she only dreams about bombs or war when there has been an explosion or bomb scare in the area. Everyday life is affected so that even a simple event such as going shopping has to be treated cautiously. It is risky, as the dream of Fran (11) indicates:

> I was doing my Christmas shopping and I bought my mummy a pair of slippers. They blew up in the taxi but somehow I got home and my mummy tried them on and her foot blew away.

This level of chilling, almost taken-for-granted adaptation to threat was underlined for me when I was last in Belfast researching this book. Deciding to have a coffee and a sandwich in a busy department store café, I asked two women if I could sit at their table. They began chatting about Christmas shopping and how full the shop was. I asked them if people were bothered by the heavy security in city-centre Belfast. 'Oh no, not really, you get used to it. The only thing is, I would never bring both my children in at once. I always leave one at home.' The other woman endorsed this practice. The ever-present fear of explosions and violence means that family activities are restricted. As they added, 'At least if we don't all go out together here, if anything happens, maybe some of the family will be safe.'

The range of powerful, destructive imagery is staggering. Claire (11), from Belfast, dreamt of helping her family of fifteen to escape after she heard the ticking of a bomb; Jane (14), from Londonderry, dreamt about her mother being shot in the back by soldiers; Anthony (14) found that his recurring nightmare was a replay of events in which a friend of his was kidnapped and taken to an empty house where stone slabs were dropped on his knees. Knee-capping happens in nightmares as well as in mean streets.

Fear inherent in everyday life finds expression in Laura's (15) dream in which the army are looking for her and when they catch her they shoot her – 'they blew me apart'. Her other nightmares are equally distressing, though the threat comes from another camp:

> I would often dream of the devil and the UVF. My next door neighbour had a bomb put in his house and he also got shot out our back. I always have awful dreams about these. And I dream they are going to kill me.

Caught in the crossfire, Laura feels safe with neither the official military nor the paramilitary group. Her waking exposure to the attempted killing of a neighbour and her everyday existence of walking along streets with gun-carrying soldiers ensures a legacy of 'awful dreams' of shootings, killings and kidnappings. Similarly, Patricia (15) dreams about terrorists coming into her house. They try to kill the family. Patricia finds that her nightmares are to do with death or people being in pain and agony.

As we have already seen, as children grow so their dreams change. If they feel more in control this is seen in the dream content. For instance, take Anne (15), from Londonderry. When she was younger she used to have many dreams of death, especially of her family, but she has noticed that as she has grown older they are more about running up hills and reaching the top. But there is still a residue of conflict present. Candidly she told me that she was a Protestant and felt very strongly about the strife she lived with day in, day out and that her friends thought her very bitter about Catholics. Her dreams are filled with men in masks shooting her father, and of her baby niece being abducted by robots. Another dream she described was about going to a big city and being taken up in an aeroplane. She then threw out bombs and blew up the city. When she woke up, she said she felt no remorse. Dream revenge on a city that has been cruel to her at least gives vent to her own anger.

People breaking in

Many children, especially those living in Belfast, told me of dreams in which someone breaks into their home. Typically the home represents a place in which we are secure, cared for and protected from the outside world. There is no such guarantee in these dreams. This reflects both anxiety felt by many inhabitants of big cities anywhere in the world but also the special situation in Belfast, where houses are subject to summary intrusion by both army and paramilitary personnel.

Shauna (11), a Catholic girl from Belfast, told me: 'I normally dream about the UVF breaking into our house and I hide behind the cupboard so that if they killed everyone else they wouldn't get me.' Her mother listens in a bemused way to most of Shauna's dreams but, she said, she takes the ones about the UVF very seriously.

Being able to accept a high level of risk is part of the price of army personnel in Ireland, as in other countries, and children in army families have many fears. Judy's (14) father is in the army and she worries about his safety:

> I have nightmares about someone coming into our house and killing my dad ... When they have killed him, they kill everyone except me and my dog. And I have to live alone in my house.

The cathartic value of dreams is already apparent to Louise who is just 11. She sees the purpose of dreaming as being 'to help ourselves relax and to help us stop being violent if our dreams are nightmares'. Her own feelings of violence are not permitted, yet why should she not feel rage that her life so far has been so deeply affected by adult problems? Her dreams are the only outlet open to her at present, living as she does in an authoritarian family where the expression of anger is seen as a sign of misbehaviour and disrespect.

She too has nightmares about people breaking into her house and shooting everyone 'and killing Ginger and Lizzie and the rest of my pets'. Pets are innocent, non-participators in conflict, as are most children. Louise projects her vulnerability on to her pets.

Hopelessness and helplessness in the face of war
There is a sense of hopelessness in many dreams of children living in Northern Ireland. A comment from an 11-year-old

from Belfast sums up his despair: 'There is nothing good to think about in this world, that is why we dream.' Pamela (13) from County Antrim explains in more detail:

> As you must realize, the conflict in Ireland makes our lives different from other teenagers, not drastically but I believe our hopes and dreams for the future cannot be compared to those of children in England and Scotland. Most of us hold no hope for the civil war's end, so we will leave Ireland.

Pamela, a clever girl doing well at school, will probably become part of the brain drain that is at present affecting Northern Ireland so badly.

In *Children of the Troubles* great attention is given to the effects that the 'troubles' have had on children from Northern Ireland. Editor Joan Harbison found that children were coping surprisingly well with the turmoil in which they live. Academically schools in Northern Ireland often out-perform their mainland counterparts in terms of examination success at 16 and beyond. School is the one place where children can receive 'rewards' for effort, which is not the case in other areas of life where they have no control.

Moya (11), like all Belfast children, has never known total peace and security in her city. For her, the abnormal has almost become the normal. She described a dream:

> The most frightening dream I have had is that nearly the whole of Belfast is in a large room but my mummy and aunt are standing outside under a lamp-post when two giant monsters come and take them away and crush them on the rocks by Belfast Lough. All the people in the room are fighting. Some old women are praying for peace between them as they are Protestants and Catholics. Then the monsters come back and crush the room with the people in it.

The amoral violence of Moya's 'monster' is not affected by fighting, nor is it affected by prayers. It continues on its path of callous destruction regardless. In her dream she has 'nearly the whole of Belfast' gathered together under one roof, and still they

cannot deflect the evil of the 'monster'. The sense of powerlessness is palpable. But what does the monster symbolize? The
war for which no one can find a solution? The fact that her
mother and aunt and all of us are helpless against a larger-than-
life force, such as God or the Devil? Or is it a projection of her
own anger? Is the monster an expression of her own feelings of
outrage towards all those adults who are supposed to know
better and be in control but who are not? She feels no one can
save her from this aggressor.

How do children cope?

A headteacher of a primary school in the heart of Belfast told
me how the children coped. Most were very resilient but the
crucial factor was the reactions of the child's mother, a view
endorsed by the research of Professor Jennifer Bryce whose
work was carried out in the Lebanon. The headteacher said,
'The stark reality of life and death, of being bombed out and
having nowhere to live, gives everything a different complexion.
But, if the mother keeps life as normal as possible, if she does
not go to pieces, then the child is OK. If the mother does go to
pieces then the child suffers badly.'

In the last twenty years many children at her school have had
a member of their family killed in the troubles; some pupils have
themselves died. The headteacher encourages the children to
mourn their loss and celebrate the short life of the dead child.
By caring, coping and honestly facing the feelings that life and
death evoke, she provides a positive model for children to
emulate. She and her fellow teachers give some experience of
normality and order in a disordered world. For these children
school is a relatively safe place in an unsafe world.

Coping with death as we saw in the last chapter is difficult
for many children, but in places like Northern Ireland it becomes
even more problematic, especially when it may seem so arbitrary.
In a study of Belfast children, Rona Fields found an obsession
with death and dying among older children. The high incidence
of dreams which include death would seem to support the idea
that it is a subject to which children from Northern Ireland are

James (9) A dream influenced by reports of conflict in Northern Ireland.

more highly sensitized. This will also reflect the fact that death rituals, such as the holding of a wake, are much more obvious there and are not treated as a taboo area as they are in much of the rest of Britain.

When children are caught up in a disaster, like adults they are affected by many factors. However, research after numerous horrific disasters in Great Britain has shown that you do not have to have suffered direct injury to be affected. People who live near to the place where a disaster happens are affected; people who help, such as firefighters, police and passers-by are affected; families of the victims are affected – the ripples spread widely.

In Northern Ireland exposure to unexpected, traumatic incidents such as bombings and shootings disturb the population. The closer the child is to the incident the worse it may be, but sustained low-level exposure also causes chronic anxiety. As we have seen earlier, symptoms of Post Traumatic Stress Syndrome include sleep disorders and nightmares. With children the response of the adults in their life, particularly the mother, is central to their successful recovery from disaster experiences; the more secure they feel the better they can cope.

For many children the response of parents to the 'troubles' has been a mixed blessing. On one hand parents, mothers predominantly, are very concerned about where their children are and insist that when a child is not at school or at a friend's house she must be at home, certainly not in the streets. That filtering out of experiences is a safety precaution and leads children to feel more protected and secure. On the other hand, however, it makes many youngsters feel curtailed and constrained. This causes conflict for many children and that is revealed in their dreams. Frequently parental anxiety is part and parcel of the whole anxious tone of the dream. Parents and children talking about the feelings helps both as a means of understanding the pressures and as a way of coping with them.

Margaret now teaches children, but as a child living through the blitz of World War II she had intense anxiety dreams. The hardest thing she felt she had to cope with was the fact that her mother never admitted having any feelings about the situation. So under control did she keep them that Margaret felt guilty for feeling afraid. One way we can avoid a repeat of this feeling of inadequacy which hampers later adult life, is to admit that we are afraid. Though we are scared we can still function and manage our lives; the admission of fear does not mean we are weak. We empower our children when we share with them.

Religious belief gives many Northern Irish children comfort and power in their dreams. Sean (11), from Belfast, has such a magical self-protective ability. In one nightmare he dreamt that his father turned into a monster, swiftly followed by all the rest of the men in his family. Sean had to find a medallion to turn them back again. The medallion of the Virgin Mary protects and saves him. In church and school he will have learnt about the power of the mother of Christ to intercede on his behalf; in his dream he calls upon it.

Play
Through play children express their knowledge of the world and attempt to master it. Through play they practise skills. However,

what we see in South Africa, Palestine, Israel and other war zones, is that children play at war. In Northern Ireland children play at being terrorists and gunmen. They play at being strong and in control. They play at having power when they are powerless. In their play with their toys children are assertive rather than passive, which is a healthy progression. By repeatedly exposing herself to the painful events of life the child hardens herself to it. Where it is successful, she has performed her own de-sensitization programme.

Encouraging children to play and to act out dreams is very useful, especially if you are on hand to join in or talk about it should the child want you to. Be directed by the child rather than tell her what to do, that way you will discover much more about how she sees the world. Play is vitally important to a child's development, indeed as Winnicott said, 'Play is the work of childhood.'

Children and families manage grief, fear and anxiety better when they are given time. They need time to talk to someone who will listen in a sensitive and supportive way. They need time to describe their nightmares and to be reassured that they are not alone, bad or mad because they have disturbing dreams. Children need help in understanding that nightmares are symptomatic of the stress under which they live.

Mastering their experiences through dream-work is another useful tool in the emotional-repair work kit. In Haifa, Ofra Ayalon works with Israeli children in classrooms, helping them to cope with their anxieties. By understanding the original traumatic events or those which may arise, such as air raids and bombings, children may no longer be overwhelmed. Although they still feel sad, they share fears and are not trapped in isolating fear. They can more easily cope with living.

Stories also can be used with children to help them cope with their fears. Ofra describes their use in her schools project and shows how, though the pain and anguish of loss still has to be lived through, talking and sharing and learning how others have come out of the other side of devastating experiences inspires others to hope and to live.

My happiest dream

Children in Northern Ireland dream of good things; there is happiness amidst the despair. As well as all the negative dream imagery we have seen so far, there are good times in dreams. Meeting fairies, eating wonderful food, dating pop stars and being bridesmaids, as well as the dreamer getting married herself, all feature. Shauna (11), who we met earlier, described her happiest dream.

> I am winning the heavy dancing championships. I am an Irish dancer and I normally dream this just before an Irish dancing festival.

Although Peggy (11) dreams of losing her family in wars, she does have heavenly dreams too:

> The happiest dream I've had is walking down the Garden of Eden in a pure white dress flowing and finding a baby wrapped in white linen.

Religious imagery abounds for Northern Irish children, as it does for Sean (11). He told me:

> I flew away to a desert island with my two sisters and the king of the sea came and lifted the island and brought us to heaven. There were angels flying and at the gate of heaven I saw angels welcoming me in.

He and his sisters, to whom he feels very close, escape earthly conflict in the streets and in the family, to a place which promises paradise.

Belfast-born Erin (11) escapes from her waking environment of burned-out hi-jacked cars and buses which litter the street on which she lives. She escapes the night-time sounds of helicopters hovering overhead and police sirens:

> My happiest dream was one where I went to fairyland and they gave me three wishes. I wished that Conall was alive (that's a baby that I minded) and when I got back from fairyland I saw him rise from his coffin. But that was only a dream.

Other forms of escapism featured strongly in dreams of these children. Going on holiday, travelling from home, being Santa's helper and having special treats were usual. Others involved having fun. Jill (10), for instance, dreamt that she had a bouncing castle at her home and she could jump from her bedroom window all day long. Others were about peace.

Wish-fulfilling peace dreams

Children, like their parents, are worn out living in a community which is so torn. They long for peace and this shows in their dreams, as Laura (15) makes clear:

> My happiest dream was that our family had lots of money. There was peace in our community and we were all wealthy and wise.

It is a dream shared with Marian (15), from Londonderry:

> I dreamt about Ireland being blown up and how the Catholics and Protestants joined forces. Although I know this will never happen.

In the latter dream, a fresh start has to be made because the old land has been destroyed.

The theme of people living in unity is often mentioned. Judy (14) had a pleasurable dream in which she fell through a hole when walking in the woods. She landed on a soft bed-like structure and: 'Everyone was happy and I was too. No one fought, everyone laughed, every animal and person lived together.' This is very similar to many of the dreams told by Asian children, as we have already seen. There is some escape from conflict, be it racial or sectarian, in dreams.

Seeing such a catalogue of dreams from children who live in places like Northern Ireland can be difficult to cope with for the adults, let alone the children. Yet the import is clear. Children are deeply affected by the wars they are forced to live. And while the external conflict rages, we need to bear in mind that these children have the same internal wars raging as children everywhere. From infancy to adolescence they struggle to learn, to become independent and to become self-directed individuals. That is a hard enough task for childhood without adding yet another externally imposed, burdensome conflict. But, whatever happens, dreams will encompass and reveal the process and progress of our children's lives.

TEN

Dream Sharing

Children enjoy talking about dreams when they trust that the listener or listeners will not ridicule them. Surprised as they sometimes are by their own dream concoctions, they often want reassurance from others that they are not weird. Dream sharing provides a chance to exchange dreams, to talk through issues they raise and to celebrate the creativity our dreams reveal.

One way to encourage understanding of dreams is to start a dream group. Those of you who work with children in settings such as residential homes, hospitals and schools where active tutorial work takes place will already know of the great insights children gain from sharing with peers. Working with dreams in a group gives children a place where their dreams are treated seriously and sensitively and children of all ages can benefit by joining in.

Starting a dream group

You have already learnt from the rest of the book about the importance of listening to what children say without passing judgements. It is so damaging for children, and adults, if you say, 'That was a bad, violent dream so you must be a violent, bloodthirsty person.' Dreams do not have a moral code, they are uncensored expressions of ideas and feelings and as such are not subject to the same waking codes. Passing negative judgements will make children feel guilty which in turn makes them clam up, refusing to talk about dreams because they are frightened of what you will say. So, bearing that in mind, what do you do if you want to start a group where children can talk about dreams?

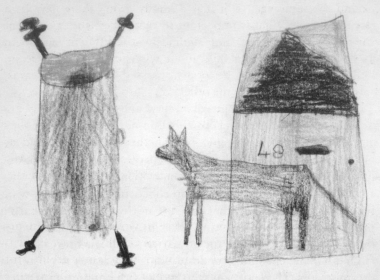

Chandra (7) Attacking animals symbolize unspoken fears in many dreams. The untamed nature of wild animals strikes an emotional chord in young children.

Think about the aim of the group

The simple aim may be to provide an opportunity for children to share dreams and to understand themselves more clearly as they understand their dreams. However, if you work with a specialized group, such as depressed children, you may need to consider what other aims you might have. In such a group, an objective might be to enable the group members to face their fears or to identify strong 'helpers' in their dreams, or to provide an opportunity for them to act out emotional aspects of their dreams which are repressed / depressed during waking life.

Time spent considering why you are setting up a group and what you hope will be achieved, is very worthwhile. It makes all the other stages much clearer and easier.

Who will be in the group?

You may decide to have a group where the children are all

around the same age, or if it is a family group there may be a spread of ages. What is important to remember is that different things are appropriate and significant to different ages. An adolescent may want to talk about why he has a wet dream, while a six-year-old may be totally obsessed by monster dreams; both may be inhibited by the other.

Different levels of language ability and understanding are factors you should consider. By this I do not mean whether they share the same mother tongue, but whether they can share ideas and appreciate what other people in the group might be getting at. Thinking out your aims should make this part much easier.

The best group size
If you want to give everyone a chance to work on dreams in any depth, then you need to keep the group small, seven or eight is enough. Having said that, you can work with larger groups, for example a whole class of children, but the level will be more superficial. In larger groups you, as the group facilitator / enabler, will not have much time to pick up the wide variety of issues that will be raised during any one session.

If you have to work with a large group give children the opportunity to talk in small groups or in pairs. Also, be aware that children may want to spend time with you if they do not understand their dreams or are troubled by what has been revealed during a dream-group session.

Decide dates and time
Clearly, the time has to be convenient for the group members. Very young children will be tired at night so that is not a good time for them. Choose a time to which everyone can make a regular commitment because it is not a good idea for people to drop in and out of the group. Obviously, people get ill and cannot attend but participants feel devalued if they are second choice to other activities such as TV programmes!

You will need to decide how long the group will run. Will it be open-ended and ongoing, or will it run for, say, ten weekly sessions? Be realistic about the time you can afford. It is useful

Christopher (6) '*Twice a giant caterpillar squashed my* house and here it is eating me.'

to have a time limit with children but there is nothing to stop you re-negotiating when the time is up. That way you have a chance to review how the group has gone and to recruit new members if old ones leave.

Dream groups for children should be run for no more than two to three hours. Longer than that is too demanding, I think, and for younger ones the sessions may be much shorter. Be guided by your knowledge of the children. Dream-work is work on our emotional selves and that is very draining, so be sensitive to signs of tiredness.

Choose a venue
The room should be welcoming with comfortable chairs arranged in a circle. It should be private and free of interruptions or onlookers. Also it is useful to have some tables, paper and paints or pencils for when you do dream drawings.

Define the boundaries
It is important to work out boundaries; firstly for you so that

you know what issues you feel comfortable with and can cope with, and it is also important for the children. Boundaries help children feel secure. So if you are running a group in a school the children need to know that it is OK, should they dream of a teacher in an uncomplimentary light, to talk about it! This and the following issues can be negotiated at the first meeting.

Confidentiality

A contract of confidentiality should be negotiated at your first meeting. Children should be encouraged to think about whether details of dreams and what comes up in the group should be secret or not. Maybe some members will say when they especially want personal information kept within the group. Whatever you negotiate about confidentiality, remember that dreams can elicit emotive, previously undisclosed material and the climate of unbroken trust is vital in such a sensitive area.

Establish ground rules

It is useful to go through this aspect with the children. At the first meeting when you have begun to set the atmosphere as one which is about having fun and learning by sharing with one another, ask the children how you as a group can best work together. Encourage open discussion and ensure everyone has a chance to say a little bit at least. Be guided by your group. In my own experience of working with groups the following are worth considering:

- We will listen whenever a person is talking,
- We will try to understand how s/he feels about the dream and not make fun or be unpleasant or unresponsive about it,
- We will share our ideas but not in a bullying way,
- We will be honest,
- We will work together.

Create the right atmosphere

A dream group should feel warm, comfortable, caring, supportive and positive. Children will feel confident when they are a valued part of the group and will flourish in a place they enjoy.

Wesley (7) A mean wolf chases Darren but Dad comes between, knocks the wolf over with his car and Darren is saved!

Everyone can participate
There are no right or wrong interpretations about dreams. There is no list that will definitively tell you what each dream means. The dream belongs to the dreamer and dream sharing helps that dreamer to understand the message for herself. So encourage everyone to join in the discussion and to listen to various points of view while ensuring that everyone understands that an explanation or interpretation has got to feel right, to resonate for the dreamer before it should be taken on board.

Children can take it in turns in the group to present a dream. This can be done by talking about it or by drawing it. In the latter case, a shy child might want to show the drawing to the group and answer questions about the dream activity rather than giving a long explanation. Be sensitive to the level of confidence of the child and always help as much as you can to bring out those children who feel ill at ease in a group.

Find a creative approach for the group
Groups are dynamic organisms, they flow and change. With this in mind find an approach that works best with your group. For

instance, some dream groups run well when at each meeting
every person has some time to talk about a dream s/he has had
in the previous week. In this way, each person has some time at
each meeting. However, this might not suit every individual's
needs.

Another approach is for the group to decide to work in
depth on one or two dreams in each session, after having a
quick survey of everyone's dreams. This can be useful if someone
has had a particularly disturbing dream and wants help in
unravelling its meaning.

A third method is more structured. With this approach you
decide what areas of dreams you want to work on or learn
about and spend a session on each. So you might devise a
programme to include animals in dreams, dream monsters,
nightmares, problem-solving in dreams and so on. In each case,
encourage the children to consult their own dream records for
relevant material and see if you can find illustrative material to
bring to the group.

Dream records

Encourage each child to keep a record of their dreams in a
special notebook. Drawings too will form part of this dream
history, and every dream should be dated. Over time a pattern
may emerge which will help the dreamer identify the purpose of
the dreams.

At the last session of a dream group it is helpful to look at the
developments that have taken place by having a kind of 'Retro-
spective Exhibition'. Sharing in the rewards of growth as well
as being part of the process leaves everyone feeling positive.

The role of the facilitator

I use the word facilitator rather than leader because the former
is one who helps in the process whereas a leader usually has a
much more directive role. The exciting aspect of dream-work is
that we never know quite where dreams will lead us and during
an exploration of a dream, insights can come from anyone.

Your role as facilitator is to provide the setting and do most of the organization and then to be a kind of conductor of the music, holding the players together to achieve the best interpretation for the dream creator. The dreamer is the composer and ultimately it is to provide a satisfactory expression of her creation that we join together. Along the way all members of the group have a chance to play, to learn and to enjoy the process and production.

Be tender: in sharing dreams we share our deepest selves. The poet Yeats captured this in 'He Wishes for the Cloths of Heaven':

> Had I the heavens' embroidered cloths,
> Enwrought with golden and silver light,
> The blue and the dim and the dark cloths
> Of night and light and the half-light,
> I would spread the cloths under your feet:
> But I, being poor, have only my dreams;
> I have spread my dreams under your feet;
> Tread softly because you tread on my dreams.

Helpful Books for Children on Dreaming and Sleeping

These books will help children to understand what dreams are and where they come from. They will help you to open up the topic of dreaming so that you can encourage children to share the joys and anxieties of their dream world.

The age divisions are merely guidelines; many books recommended for younger readers will also be suitable for much older children. You know your child best so be guided by that knowledge.

Age five and under

Arnold, Tedd, *No Jumping on the Bed*, Bodley Head, 1987.

Bell Corfield, Robin, *Somebody's Sleepy*, Bodley Head, 1988.

Brown, Ruth, *Our Cat Flossie*, Andersen Press, 1988.

Collington, P., *The Angel and the Soldier Boy*, Magnet Books, 1988.

Gay, Marie-Louise, *Moonbeam on a Cat's Ear*, Picture Lions, 1987.

Hague, K., *Out of the Nursery, Into the Night*, Methuen, 1987.

Hill, S., *One Night at a Time*, Picture Lions, 1986.

Howard, Jane, *When I'm Sleepy*, Andersen Press, 1988.

Hutchins, Pat, *Good-Night, Owl!*, Bodley Head, 1987.

Johnson, Jane, *My Bedtime Rhyme*, Andersen Press, 1988.

Kitmura, Sartoshi, *When Sheep Cannot Sleep*, Beaver Books, 1988.

Lloyd, Errol, *Nandy's Bedtime*, Bodley Head, 1982.

Omerod, Jan, *Moonlight*, Kestrel Books, 1982.

Age five to nine

Carroll, Lewis, *Alice's Adventures in Wonderland*, Puffin, 1989.
Foreman, Michael, *Land of Dreams*, Andersen Press, 1982.
Goode, Diane, *I Hear a Noise*, Andersen Press, 1988.
Impey, Rose, *The Flat Man*, Ragged Bears, 1988.
Jones, Ann, *The Quilt*, Julia MacRae Books, 1984.
Marshall, Margaret, *Mike*, Bodley Head, 1983.
Mayer, M., *There's a Nightmare in my Cupboard*, Methuen, 1983.
Mayle, P., *Sweet Dreams and Monsters*, Macmillan, 1987.
Pavey, P., *One Dragon's Dream*, Puffin, 1981.
Pelgrom, Els, *Little Sophie and Lanky Flop*, Jonathan Cape, 1988.
Pinkney, Jerry, *Half a Moon and One Whole Star*, Bodley Head, 1987.
Pinkney, Jerry, *The Patchwork Quilt*, Bodley Head, 1985.
Pomeranz, Charlotte, *All Asleep*, Julia MacRae Books, 1985.
Richardson, Jean, *Beware, Beware*, Hamish Hamilton, 1987.
Richardson, John, *The Dreambeast*, Andersen Press, 1988.
Riddell, Chris, *Mr Underbed*, Andersen Press, 1988.
Ross, T., *Naughty Nigel*, Puffin, 1988.
Sendak, Maurice, *In the Night Kitchen*, Puffin, 1973.
Sendak, Maurice, *Where the Wild Things Are*, Bodley Head, 1975.
Seuss, Dr, *Sleep Book*, Collins, 1962.
Simmons, Posy, *Fred*, Jonathan Cape, 1987.
Wahl, J., *Humphrey's Bear*, Gollancz, 1988.
Wild, M., *There's a Sea in my Bedroom*, Hamish Hamilton, 1984.
Yabuuchi, Masayuki, *Sleeping Animals*, Bodley Head, 1983.

Age eleven and over

Blume, Judy, *Letters to Judy*, Pan, 1986.
Dickinson, Peter, *Merlin Dreams*, Gollancz, 1988.
Duncan, Lois, *Stranger with My Face*, Hamish Hamilton, 1983.

Lindsay, Rae, *Sleep and Dreams*, Franklin Watts, New York, 1978.

Melling, O. R., *The Singing Stone*, Puffin, 1986.

Osborne, Victor, *Moondream*, Piper / Heinemann, 1988.

Storr, Catherine, *Marianne Dreams*, Puffin, 1964.

Bibliography

Book publishers are located in London unless otherwise stated.

Chapter 1

Ablon, S. L., and Mach, J. E., 'Children's Dreams Reconsidered', *The Psychoanalytic Study of the Child Series*, No. 35, 1980.

Catalano, S. J., 'Children's Dreams: Their Use in Clinical Practice', *Child Adolescent Social Work Journal*, Vol. 1, Part 4, 1984.

Evans, Christopher, *Landscapes of the Night*, edited and completed by Peter Evans, Gollancz, 1983.

Freud, S., *The Interpretation of Dreams*, Harmondsworth, Penguin, 1976.

Greenberg, R., and Pearlman, C., 'REM sleep and the analytic process: a psycho-physiologic bridge', *Report to the American Psychoanalytical Association*, New York, 1972.

Hartmann, E., *The Functions of Sleep*, New Haven, Yale University Press, 1973.

Luce, G. G., and Segal, J., *Sleep*, New York, Coward, McCann & Geoghegan, 1966.

Mackie, Robin, 'Is the 24-hour day really such a wild dream?', *The Times Higher Education Supplement*, 29 May 1981.

Rossi, E. R., 'Psychosynthesis and the New Biology of Dreams and Psychotherapy', *American Journal of Psychotherapy*, Vol. 27, No. 1, 1973.

Siva Sankar, D. V. (ed.), *Mental Health in Children*, New York, P J D Publications, 1976.

Chapter 2

Bakwin, H., and Bakwin, R. M., *Behavior Disorders in Children*, Philadelphia, Saunders, 1972.

Bidder, R. T., Gray, O. P., Howells, P. M., and Eaton, M. P., 'Sleep Problems in Pre-school Children: Community Clinics', *Child*, Vol. 12, 1986.

Crick, F., and Mitchison, G., 'The Function of Dream Sleep', *Nature*, Vol. 304, 1984.

Empson, J., 'Waking up to the truth about sleep', *Guardian*, 31 May 1984.

Fordham, M., *The Life of Childhood*, Kegan Paul, 1944.

Foulkes, D., 'Children's Dreams: Age Changes and Sex Differences', *Waking and Sleeping*, Vol. 1, 1977.

Harms, E. (ed.), *Problems of Sleep and Dreams in Children*, Pergamon Press, 1964.

Jung, C. G., *Man and His Symbols*, Aldus Books, 1964.

Knopf, I. J., *Childhood Psychopathology*, New Jersey, Prentice Hall, 1984.

Kohler, W. C., Coddington, R. D., and Agnew, H. W., 'Sleep Patterns in Two-year-old Children', *Journal of Pediatrics*, Vol. 72, 1968.

Masson, J. M., *The Assault on Truth*, Harmondsworth, Penguin, 1984.

Siva Sankar, D. V. (ed.), *Mental Health in Children*, New York, P J D Publications, 1976.

Schwartz, S., and Johnson, J. H., *Psychopathology of Childhood*, New York, Pergamon Press, 1985.

Chapter 3

Ames, Louise Bates, 'Sleep and Dreams in Childhood' in Ernest Harms (ed.), *Problems of Sleep and Dreams in Children*, Pergamon Press, 1964.

Cirlot, J. E., *A Dictionary of Symbols*, Routledge & Kegan Paul, 1962.

Faber, A., and Mazlish, E., *Siblings Without Rivalry*, New York, Avon Books, 1987.

Foulkes, D., 'Children's Dreams: Age Changes and Sex Differences', *Waking and Sleeping*, Vol. 1, 1977.

Kimmins, C. W., *Children's Dreams*, Longmans, Green & Co., 1920.

Mallon, B., *Women Dreaming*, Fontana, 1987.

Terr, Lenore C., 'Nightmares in Children' in C. Guilleminault (ed.), *Sleep and its Disorders in Children*, New York, Raven Press, 1987.

Winnicott, D. W., *Home is Where We Start From*, Harmondsworth, Penguin, 1987.

Chapter 4

Blume Judy, *Letters to Judy: What Kids Wish They Could Tell You*, Pan, 1987.

Dowling, Colette, *The Cinderella Complex*, Fontana, 1981.

Foulkes, D., 'Children's Dreams: Age Changes and Sex Differences', *Waking and Sleeping*, Vol. 1, 1977.

Guardian, 'Insult to Injury' (NSPCC figures on abuse), 12 October 1988.

Karpman, S. B., 'Fairy Tales and Script Drama Analysis', *Transactional Analysis Bulletin*, Vol. 7, No. 2, April 1968.

Leach, D. J., and Raybould, E. C., *Learning and Behaviour Difficulties in School*, Open Books, 1977.

Norwood, Robin, *Women Who Love Too Much*, Arrow Books, 1985.

O'Donnell, M., 'Suicide Mission', *Guardian*, 19 December 1984.

Parker, Sharon D., RN MSN, 'Accident or Suicide? Do life-changing events lead to adolescent suicide?' *Journal of Psychological Nursing*, Vol. 26, No. 6, 1988.

Sirois-Berliss, Michelle, and de Koninck, Joseph, 'Menstrual stress and Dreams: Adaptation or Interference?', *Psychiatric Journal of University of Ottowa*, Vol. 7, No. 2, June 1982.

Skynner, R., and Cleese, J., *Families and How To Survive Them*, Methuen, 1987.

Terr, Lenore C., 'Nightmares in Children' in C. Guilleminault (ed.), *Sleep and Its Disorders in Children*, New York, Raven Press, 1987.

Yamamoto, K., Soliman, A., Parsons, J., and Davies, O. L., 'Voices in Unison: Stressful Events in the Lives of Children from Six Countries', *Journal of Child Psychology and Psychiatry*, Vol. 28, No. 6, 1987.

Chapter 5

Balbernie, R., 'Are They Trying To Kill Me?', *New Society*, 25 October 1985.

Bertoia, J., and Allan, J., 'Counselling Seriously Ill Children: Use of Spontaneous Drawings', *Elementary School Guidance and Counselling*, Vol. 22, No. 3, February 1988.

Burton, Dr Lindy, 'Anxiety Relating to Illness and Treatment' in Ved P. Varma (ed.), *Anxiety in Children*, Croom Helm, 1984.

Droske, S. C., 'Children's Behavioural Changes Following Hospitalization – Have We Prepared the Patient?' *Institute for the Association for the Care of Children in Hospitals*, Vol. 7, No. 2, 1978.

Feinberg, I., 'Eye movement activity during sleep and intellectual function in mental retardation', *Science*, No. 159, 1968.

Franz, M.-L. von, 'Archetypes Surrounding Death', *Quadrant*, Vol. 12, No. 5, 1979.

Goodwin, J., 'Use of Drawings in Evaluating Children Who May Be Incest Victims', *Children and Youth Services Review*, Vol. 4, 1982.

Handler, L., 'Amelioration of Nightmares in Children', *Psychotherapy Theory, Research and Practice*, Vol. 9, 1972.

Hartmann, E., Baekeland, F., Zwilling, G., and Hoy, P., 'Sleep Need: How Much and What Kind?', *American Journal of Psychiatry*, Vol. 127, 1971.

Jastrow, J., 'The Dreams of the Blind', *New Princeton Review*, Vol. 5, 1988.

Kirtley, D. D., *The Psychology of Blindness*, Chicago, Nelson-Hall, 1975.

Kraft, I., 'Use of Dreams in Adolescent Psychotherapy', *Psychotherapy: Theory, Research and Practice*, Vol. 6, No. 2, 1969.

Kübler-Ross, E., *On Children and Death*, New York, Macmillan, 1983.

Levitan, H., 'Dreams which Precede Asthma Attacks' in Krakowski, Adam J., and Kimball, Chase P. (eds), *Psychosomatic Medicine: Theoretical, Clinical and Transcultural Aspects*, New York, Plenum, 1988.

Levy, D., 'Psychic Trauma of Operations in Children and a Note on Combat Neurosis', *American Journal of the Disturbed Child*, Vol. 69, 1945.

Maisch, H., *Incest*, New York, Stein & Day, 1973.

Petrillo, M., and Sanger, S., *Emotional Care of Hospitalized Children*, 2nd Edn, Philadelphia, J. B. Lippincott Co., 1980.

Rossi, E., 'Psychosynthesis and the New Biology of Dreams and Psychotherapy', *American Journal of Psychotherapy*, Vol. 27, No. 1, 1973.

Sabini, Meredith, 'Dreams as an Aid in Determining Diagnosis, Prognosis and Attitude Towards Treatment', *Psychotherapy and Psychosomatics*, Vol. 36, 1981.

Scott, E. M., 'The Occurrence of the Isakower Phenomena in an Alcoholic Patient', *Alcoholism Today Quarterly*, Vol. 3, No. 4, 1986.

Smith, R. C., 'A Possible Biologic Role of Dreaming', *Psychotherapy and Psychosomatics*, Vol. 41, Part 4, 1984.

Van de Castle, R. L., 'His, Hers and the Children's', *Psychology Today*, June 1970.

Weiss, J. Volck, 'Dreaming and Night Asthma in Children', unpublished Ph.D. thesis, University of Denver, June 1969.

Wolpert Burgess, A., and Lytle Holmstrom, L., 'Sexual Trauma of Children and Adolescents', *Nursing Clinics of North America*, Vol. 10, No. 3, September 1975.

Yudkin, S., 'Children and Death', *Lancet*, 7 January 1967.

Chapter 6

Barker, J. C., 'Premonitions of the Aberfan Disaster', *Journal of the Society for Psychical Research*, Vol. 44, 1967.

Blackmore, S., 'A Study of OOBE', *Journal of the Society for Psychical Research*, Vol. 51, Part 79, 1982.

Cooke, A. H., *Out of the Mouth of Babes: ESP in Children*, James Clarke & Co., 1968.

Evans, Christopher, *Landscapes of the Night*, edited and completed by Peter Evans, Gollancz, 1983.

Freud, S., *The Interpretation of Dreams*, Harmondsworth, Penguin, 1952.

Garfield, P., *Creative Dreaming*, Futura, 1976.

Green, C., *Lucid Dreams*, Institute of Psychophysical Research, 1982.

Gurney, E., *et al.*, 'Phantasms of the Living', *Society for Physical Research*, 1886.

Hearne, K., 'Control Your Own Dreams', *New Scientist*, 24 September 1981.

Inglis, B., *The Power of Dreams*, Paladin, 1988.

Jung, C. G., *Memories, Dreams, Reflections*, New York, Pantheon, 1963.

Knox-Mawr, J., 'Snuggle Under the Duvet and Devise Your Own Dreams', *Listener*, 20 January 1983.

Myers, F. W. H., *Human Personality and its Survival of Bodily Death*, Longmans, Green & Co., 1903.

Prasad, I., and Stevenson, I., 'A survey of spontaneous psychical experiences in school children of Uttar Pradesh, India', *International Journal of Paraspsychology*, Vol. 10, 1968.

Stekel, Wilhelm, *The Interpretation of Dreams*, New York, Liveright, 1943.

Targs, R., and Harary, K., *The Mind Race*, New English Library, 1984.

Ullman, M., Krippner, S., and Feldstein, S., 'Experimentally Induced Telepathic Dreams' in G. Schmeidler (ed.), *Extrasensory Perceptions*, New York, Atherton Press, 1969.

Ullman, M., and Zimmerman, N., *Working with Dreams*, New York, Dell, 1979.

Van de Castle, R., *The Psychology of Dreaming*, Morristown, New Jersey, General Learning Press, 1971.

Wolman, B. (ed.), *Handbook of Dreams: Research, Theories and Applications*, New York, Van Nostrand Reinhold, 1979.

Woods, R. K., *The World of Dreams*, New York, Random House, 1947.

Zohar, D., *Through the Time Barrier: A Study in Precognition and Modern Physics*, Paladin, 1983.

Chapter 7

Bettelheim, B., *The Uses of Enchantment: The Meaning and Importance of Fairy Tales*, Peregrine, 1978.

Blume, Judy, *Letters to Judy*, Pan, 1986.

Eron, L. D., and Huesmann, L. R., 'Television Violence and Aggressive Behaviour', in B. Lahey and A. Kazin (eds), *Advances in Clinical Child Psychology*, Vol. 7, New York, Plenum, 1984.

Fountain, Nigel, 'News Round Up', *Guardian*, 14 September 1988.

Guardian, 'Guns in the Blackboard Jungle', report of SOSAD (Save Our Sons And Daughters) parents' group, 20 January 1988.

Harries, Richard, 'The Hollow Centre of Soap Operas', *Observer*, 3 April 1988.

Herbert, Hugh, 'Comfort for Most of the People, Most of the Time', *Guardian*, 13 February 1988.

Kiley, Dan, *The Peter Pan Syndrome*, Corgi, 1984.

Kittrell, E., 'Children and Television' in P. J. Mussen *et al.* (eds), *Readings in Child and Adolescent Psychology*, New York, Harper & Row, 1980.

Lang, Cynthia, 'Children's Fears', *Parents*, USA, May 1979.

Messenger Davies, Marie, 'Red Alert for the Invasion of the Culture Snatchers', *Guardian*, 18 July 1988.

Observer, 'Co-op Ban on Guns', 19 June 1988.

Postman, N., 'Violence: A Symptom and a Cause', *Sunday Times*, 25 September 1988.

Weiser, M. G., 'Young Children and the Quality of Life', report of XVIIIth World Conference of OMEP (World Organization of Early Childhood Education).

Yule, Valerie, 'Violence and Imagination', *New Society*, 28 June 1985.

Chapter 8

Bass, E., and Thornton, L. (eds), *I Never Told Anyone: Writings by Women Survivors of Child Sexual Abuse*, New York, Harper & Row, 1983.

Bettelheim, B., *A Good Enough Parent*, Thames & Hudson, 1987.

Bowlby, John, *A Secure Base*, Routledge, 1988.

Bowlby, John, *Loss, Sadness and Depression*, Hogarth Press, 1980.

Campbell, B., *Unofficial Secrets: Child Sexual Abuse: The Cleveland Case*, Virago, 1988.

Cohen, Felice, 'Art Therapy after Accidental Death of a Sibling' in C. F. Shaefer and H. L. Millman (eds), *Therapies for Children*, New York, Joscy-Bass, 1978.

Davis, Gwynn, and Roberts, Marian, *Access to Agreement: A Consumer Study of Mediation in Family Disputes*, Oxford, OUP, 1988.

Garfield, Patricia, 'Nightmares in the Sexually Abused Female Teenager', *Psychiatric Journal of the University of Ottowa*, June 1987.

Heatherington, M., *et al.*, 'The Aftermath of Divorce' in P. H. Mussen (ed.), *Readings in Child and Adolescent Psychology*, New York, Harper & Row, 1980.

Kübler-Ross, E., *On Children and Death*, New York, Macmillan, 1983.

Mallon, Brenda, *Women Dreaming*, Fontana, 1987.

Myers, Barbara, 'To My Father' in B. McComb Jones *et al.* (eds), *Sexual Abuse of Children. Selected Readings*, Washington, Department of Health and Human Sciences, Publication No. 78-30161, 1980.

NSPCC Training Department, 'Yo-Yo Children – A Study of 23 Violent Matrimonial Cases', 1974.

Parker, Sharon D., RN, MSN, 'Accident or Suicide? Do life-changing events lead to adolescent suicide', *Journal of Psychological Nursing*, Vol. 26, No. 6, 1988.

Roith, Estelle, 'Freudian Errors', *Observer*, 20 November 1988.

Shearer, Ann, 'Society Tomorrow', *Guardian*, 22 July 1987.

Wallerstein, J., and Kelly, J. B., *Surviving the Break-up: How Children and Parents Cope with Divorce*, Grant McIntyre, 1980.

Wells, R., *Helping Children Cope with Grief*, Sheldon Press, 1988.

Worden, J. W., *Grief Counselling and Grief Therapy*, Tavistock Publications, 1983.

Yacoubian, J. T., and Lourie, R. S., 'Suicide and Attempted Suicide in Children and Adolescents' in S. L. Copel (ed.), *Behaviour Pathology of Childhood and Adolescence*, New York, Basic Books, 1973.

Chapter 9

Ayalon, Ofra, *Rescue: Community Orientated Preventive Education* (COPE), Haifa, Nord Publications, 1987.

Bryce, Jennifer, *Cries of the Children of Lebanon*, UNICEF, 1986.

Cairns, E., *Caught in the Crossfire*, New York, Appletree Press, 1987.

Chivian, E., *The Human Cost of Nuclear War*, Medical Campaign Against Nuclear Weapons, Titan Press, 1983.

Chivian, E., and Snow, R., 'There's A Nuclear War Going On Inside Me' (transcript of videotape of classroom discussion with 6- to 10-year-old children in USA).

Donnelly, Frances, 'The Biggest Irish Exodus Since the Potato Famine', *Listener*, 25 November 1982.

Fields, Rona, 'Psychological Genocide: The Children of Northern Ireland', *Journal of Psychohistory*, Vol. 3, Part 201–114, 1975.

Gelman, David, 'Treating War's Psychic Wounds', *Newsweek*, 29 August 1987.

Guardian, 'School Gets Radiation Pills', 5 February 1987.

Guardian, 'War Neurosis Hits Children' (report commissioned by Prince Talal bin Abdul-Aziz, Saudi Arabia, into the effects of civil war in the Lebanon), 8 October 1986.

Guardian, 'What Are You Worried About?' (Young Guardian Survey results), 7 January 1987.

Harbison, J. (ed.), *Children of the Troubles*, Stranmillis College Belfast, Learning Resources Unit, 1983.

Jahoda, G., and Harrison, S., 'Belfast Children: Some Effects of a Conflict Environment', *Irish Journal of Psychology*, Vol. 3, Part 1, 1975.

Jenvey, S., 'Sons and Haters; Ulster Youth in Conflict', *New Society*, No. 21, 1972.

Kübler-Ross, E., *On Children and Death*, New York, Macmillan, 1983.

Medical Campaign Against Nuclear Weapons, *Even Before the Bomb Drops*, 1988.

Neustatter, Angela, 'War's Grisly Toy Box', *Observer*, 18 September 1988.

Radford, Tim, 'Young Living in Fear of Nuclear War', *Guardian*, 25 April 1988.

Rosenblatt, Roger, *Children of War*, New York, Anchor Press / Doubleday, 1983.

Russell, J. L., 'Socialization and Conflict', unpublished Ph.D. thesis, University of Strathclyde, 1974.

Thompson, James, *The Psychological Aspects of Nuclear War*, New York, Wiley, 1985.

Thompson, K., *Under Siege: Racism and Violence in Britain*, Harmondsworth, Penguin, 1988.

Waterson, Tony, 'Children and the Threat of Nuclear War', *Lancet*, 13 June 1987.

Wicks, Ben, *No Time to Wave Goodbye*, Bloomsbury, 1988.

Winnicott, D. W., *Playing and Reality*, Harmondsworth, Penguin, 1974.

Wolfenstein, M. *Disaster*, Illinois, The Free Press, 1957.

Chapter 10

Mallon, Brenda, *An Introduction to Counselling Skills for Special Educational Needs: Participants' Manual*, Manchester, Manchester University Press, 1987.

Shohet, R., *Dream Sharing*, Turnstone Press, 1985.

Ullman, M., and Zimmermann, N., *Working with Dreams*, New York, Dell, 1979.

Williams, S. K., *The Dreamwork Manual*, Aquarian Press, 1984.

Yeats, W. B., *Selected Poetry*, ed. A. N. Jeffares, Pan, 1962.

Index

FOR THE BEST IN PAPERBACKS, LOOK FOR THE

In every corner of the world, on every subject under the sun, Penguin represents quality and variety – the very best in publishing today.

For complete information about books available from Penguin – including Pelicans, Puffins, Peregrines and Penguin Classics – and how to order them, write to us at the appropriate address below. Please note that for copyright reasons the selection of books varies from country to country.

In the United Kingdom: Please write to *Dept E.P., Penguin Books Ltd, Harmondsworth, Middlesex, UB7 0DA*

If you have any difficulty in obtaining a title, please send your order with the correct money, plus ten per cent for postage and packaging, to *PO Box No 11, West Drayton, Middlesex*

In the United States: Please write to *Dept BA, Penguin, 299 Murray Hill Parkway, East Rutherford, New Jersey 07073*

In Canada: Please write to *Penguin Books Canada Ltd, 2801 John Street, Markham, Ontario L3R 1B4*

In Australia: Please write to the *Marketing Department, Penguin Books Australia Ltd, P.O. Box 257, Ringwood, Victoria 3134*

In New Zealand: Please write to the *Marketing Department, Penguin Books (NZ) Ltd, Private Bag, Takapuna, Auckland 9*

In India: Please write to *Penguin Overseas Ltd, 706 Eros Apartments, 56 Nehru Place, New Delhi, 110019*

In Holland: Please write to *Penguin Books Nederland B.V., Postbus 195, NL–1380AD Weesp, Netherlands*

In Germany: Please write to *Penguin Books Ltd, Friedrichstrasse 10–12, D–6000 Frankfurt Main 1, Federal Republic of Germany*

In Spain: Please write to *Longman Penguin España, Calle San Nicolas 15, E–28013 Madrid, Spain*

In France: Please write to *Penguin Books Ltd, 39 Rue de Montmorency, F-75003, Paris, France*

In Japan: Please write to *Longman Penguin Japan Co Ltd, Yamaguchi Building, 2–12–9 Kanda Jimbocho, Chiyoda-Ku, Tokyo 101, Japan*

A CHOICE OF PENGUINS

A Better Class of Person   John Osborne

The playwright's autobiography, 1929–56. 'Splendidly enjoyable' – John Mortimer. 'One of the best, richest and most bitterly truthful autobiographies that I have ever read' – Melvyn Bragg

Out of Africa   Karen Blixen (Isak Dinesen)

After the failure of her coffee-farm in Kenya, where she lived from 1913 to 1931, Karen Blixen went home to Denmark and wrote this unforgettable account of her experiences. 'No reader can put the book down without some share in the author's poignant farewell to her farm' – *Observer*

In My Wildest Dreams   Leslie Thomas

The autobiography of Leslie Thomas, author of *The Magic Army* and *The Dearest and the Best*. From Barnardo boy to original virgin soldier, from apprentice journalist to famous novelist, it is an amazing story. 'Hugely enjoyable' – *Daily Express*

The Winning Streak   Walter Goldsmith and David Clutterbuck

Marks and Spencer, Saatchi and Saatchi, United Biscuits, G.E.C. . . The U.K.'s top companies reveal their formulas for success, in an important and stimulating book that no British manager can afford to ignore.

Mind Tools   Rudy Rucker

Information is the master concept of the computer age, which throws a completely new light on the age-old concepts of space and number, logic and infinity. In *Mind Tools* Rudy Rucker has produced the most charming and challenging intellectual carnival since *Gödel, Escher, Bach*.

Bird of Life, Bird of Death   Jonathan Evan Maslow

In the summer of 1983 Jonathan Maslow set out to find the quetzal. In doing so, he placed himself between the natural and unnatural histories of Central America, between the vulnerable magnificence of nature and the terrible destructiveness of man. 'A wonderful book' – *The New York Times Book Review*

Adieux: A Farewell to Sartre Simone de Beauvoir

A devastatingly frank account of the last years of Sartre's life, and his death, by the woman who for more than half a century shared that life. 'A true labour of love, there is about it a touching sadness, a mingling of the personal with the impersonal and timeless which Sartre himself would surely have liked and understood' – *Listener*

Business Wargames James Barrie

How did BMW overtake Mercedes? Why did Laker crash? How did MacDonalds grab the hamburger market? Drawing on the tragic mistakes and brilliant victories of military history, this remarkable book draws countless fascinating parallels with case histories from industry world-wide.

Metamagical Themas Douglas R. Hofstadter

This astonishing sequel to the bestselling, Pulitzer Prize-winning *Gödel, Escher, Bach* swarms with 'extraordinary ideas, brilliant fables, deep philosophical questions and Carrollian word play' – Martin Gardner

Into the Heart of Borneo Redmond O'Hanlon

'Perceptive, hilarious and at the same time a serious natural-history journey into one of the last remaining unspoilt paradises' – *New Statesman* 'Consistently exciting, often funny and erudite without ever being over-whelming' – *Punch*

The Assassination of Federico García Lorca Ian Gibson

Lorca's 'crime' was his antipathy to pomposity, conformity and intolerance. His punishment was murder. Ian Gibson reveals the truth about Lorca's death and the atmosphere in Spain that allowed it to happen.

The Secrets of a Woman's Heart Hilary Spurling

The later life of Ivy Compton-Burnett 1920–69. 'A biographical triumph . . . elegant, stylish, witty tender, immensely acute – dazzles and exhilarates . . . a great achievement' – Kay Dick in the *Literary Review*. 'One of the most important literary biographies of the century' – *New Statesman*

FOR THE BEST IN PAPERBACKS, LOOK FOR THE

A CHOICE OF PENGUINS

Fantastic Invasion   Patrick Marnham

Explored and exploited, Africa has carried a different meaning for each wave of foreign invaders – from ivory traders to aid workers. Now, in the crisis that has followed Independence, which way should Africa turn? 'A courageous and brilliant effort' – Paul Theroux

Jean Rhys: Letters 1931–66
Edited by Francis Wyndham and Diana Melly

'Eloquent and invaluable . . . her life emerges, and with it a portrait of an unexpectedly indomitable figure' – Marina Warner in the *Sunday Times*

Among the Russians   Colin Thubron

One man's solitary journey by car across Russia provides an enthralling and revealing account of the habits and idiosyncrasies of a fascinating people. 'He sees things with the freshness of an innocent and the erudition of a scholar' – *Daily Telegraph*

The Amateur Naturalist   Gerald Durrell with Lee Durrell

'Delight . . . on every page . . . packed with authoritative writing, learning without pomposity . . . it represents a real bargain' – *The Times Educational Supplement*. 'What treats are in store for the average British household' – *Books and Bookmen*

The Democratic Economy   Geoff Hodgson

Today, the political arena is divided as seldom before. In this exciting and original study, Geoff Hodgson carefully examines the claims of the rival doctrines and exposes some crucial flaws.

They Went to Portugal   Rose Macaulay

An exotic and entertaining account of travellers to Portugal from the pirate-crusaders, through poets, aesthetes and ambassadors, to the new wave of romantic travellers. A wonderful mixture of literature, history and adventure, by one of our most stylish and seductive writers.

PENGUIN HEALTH

Audrey Eyton's F-Plus   Audrey Eyton

'Your short cut to the most sensational diet of the century' – *Daily Express*

Baby and Child   Penelope Leach

A beautifully illustrated and comprehensive handbook on the first five years of life. 'It stands head and shoulders above anything else available at the moment' – Mary Kenny in the *Spectator*

Woman's Experience of Sex   Sheila Kitzinger

Fully illustrated with photographs and line drawings, this book explores the riches of women's sexuality at every stage of life. 'A book which any mother could confidently pass on to her daughter – and her partner too' – *Sunday Times*

Food Additives   Erik Millstone

Eat, drink and be worried? Erik Millstone's hard-hitting book contains powerful evidence about the massive risks being taken with the health of the consumer. It takes the lid off the food we have and the food industry.

Living with Allergies   Dr John McKenzie

At least 20% of the population suffer from an allergic disorder at some point in their lives and this invaluable book provides accurate and up-to-date information about the condition, where to go for help, diagnosis and cure – and what we can do to help ourselves.

Living with Stress   Cary L. Cooper, Rachel D. Cooper and Lynn H. Eaker

Stress leads to more stress, and the authors of this helpful book show why low levels of stress are desirable and how best we can achieve them in today's world. Looking at those most vulnerable, they demonstrate ways of breaking the vicious circle that can ruin lives.

PENGUIN HEALTH

The Prime of Your Life Dr Miriam Stoppard

The first comprehensive, fully illustrated guide to healthy living for people aged fifty and beyond, by top medical writer and media personality, Dr Miriam Stoppard.

A Good Start Louise Graham

Factual and practical, full of tips on providing a healthy and balanced diet for young children, *A Good Start* is essential reading for all parents.

How to Get Off Drugs Ira Mothner and Alan Weitz

This book is a vital contribution towards combating drug addiction in Britain in the eighties. For drug abusers, their families and their friends.

Naturebirth Danaë Brook

A pioneering work which includes suggestions on diet and health, exercises and many tips on the 'natural' way to prepare for giving birth in a joyful relaxed way.

Pregnancy Dr Jonathan Scher and Carol Dix

Containing the most up-to-date information on pregnancy – the effects of stress, sexual intercourse, drugs, diet, late maternity and genetic disorders – this book is an invaluable and reassuring guide for prospective parents.

Care of the Dying Richard Lamerton

It is never true that 'nothing more can be done' for the dying. This book shows us how to face death without pain, with humanity, with dignity and in peace.

FOR THE BEST IN PAPERBACKS, LOOK FOR THE

PENGUIN HEALTH

Medicines: A Guide for Everybody   Peter Parish

This sixth edition of a comprehensive survey of all the medicines available over the counter or on prescription offers clear guidance for the ordinary reader as well as invaluable information for those involved in health care.

Pregnancy and Childbirth   Sheila Kitzinger

A complete and up-to-date guide to physical and emotional preparation for pregnancy – a must for all prospective parents.

The Penguin Encyclopaedia of Nutrition   John Yudkin

This book cuts through all the myths about food and diets to present the real facts clearly and simply. 'Everyone should buy one' – *Nutrition News and Notes*

The Parents' A to Z   Penelope Leach

For anyone with a child of 6 months, 6 years or 16 years, this guide to all the little problems involved in their health, growth and happiness will prove reassuring and helpful.

Jane Fonda's Workout Book

Help yourself to better looks, superb fitness and a whole new approach to health and beauty with this world-famous and fully illustrated programme of diet and exercise advice.

Alternative Medicine   Andrew Stanway

Dr Stanway provides an objective and practical guide to thirty-two alternative forms of therapy – from Acupuncture and the Alexander Technique to Macrobiotics and Yoga.